Celebrations

Celebrations

A Joyous Guide to the

Holidays from Past to Present

Jim McCann and *Jeanne Benedict*

Frank

Enjoy.

Jim McC

HPBooks

Most HPBooks are available at special quantity discounts for bulk purchases for sales promotions, premiums, fund-raising or educational use. Special books, or book excerpts, can also be created to fit specific needs.

For details, write: Special Markets, The Berkley Publishing Group, 375 Hudson Street, New York, New York 10014.

HPBooks
Published by The Berkley Publishing Group
A division of Penguin Putnam Inc.
375 Hudson Street
New York, New York 10014

Copyright © 2001 by Jim McCann and Jeanne Benedict
Text design by Richard Oriolo
Jacket design by Charles Björklund and Dorothy Wachtenheim
Jacket photo © Stockfood/Eising
Interior Photo Design: Jeanne Benedict
Interior Photo Shoot Art Direction: John Sparano
Photographer: Eddie Garcia
Photographer's Assistant: Jeff Hamilton
Food Styling: Eric Roth
Assistant Food Stylist: Hope Shapiro
Floral Stylist: 1-800-FLOWERS/Kerry Bedwell
Photo Crew: Brandon Meyer and Brady Spindel

FIRST EDITION: November 2001
Published simultaneously in Canada.

Visit our website at www.penguinputnam.com

LIBRARY OF CONGRESS CATALOGING-IN-PUBLICATION DATA

McCann, Jim
      Celebrations : a joyous guide to the holidays from past to present / Jim McCann and Jeanne
Benedict.—1st ed.
          p. cm
      Includes index.
      ISBN 1-55788-373-4
          1. Holidays—History.   2. Holiday decorations.   3. Holiday cookery.   I. Benedict, Jeanne.
    II. Title
GT3930 .M42 2001
394.26—dc21
                                                                          2001039414

Printed in the United States of America

10 9 8 7 6 5 4 3 2 1

Jim: To my parents, for teaching me

the importance of celebrations.

Jeanne: To my mother and father for giving me

happy holidays and a great childhood.

Contents

Acknowledgments

First of all, we have to acknowledge our dear family, friends, and the many associates with whom we work and play. You have always been there to help us enjoy the precious moments of our lives, and so we celebrate *you* and look forward to many more happy occasions!

Our most sincere thanks and appreciation is extended to all who helped put the book together from start to finish. We offer a warm thank-you to the charming John Duff and the lovely Lisa Queen, who brought us together for this project. Much gratitude goes out to Ken Young, Marion Rosenfeld, Kelly Mitchell, Patty Altadonna, Diane McGurrin and Jeanette Egan, whose great ideas helped sculpt the work and whose effort was immeasurable. There are not enough thank-yous for the fabulous photo shoot team who worked tirelessly while we finagled and tweaked for the perfect shot including John Sparano, Eddie Garcia, Jeff Hamilton, Sharon Bonney, Eric Roth, Hope Shapiro, Kerry Bedwell, Jaime Castellanos, Brandon Meyer, Brady Spindel, and Dan Benedict. Thank you to Susan Borgeson and Karen and Jonathon Mandell who donated their homes, and to Charles & Charles, House of Props, Lennie Marvin, Green Set, Omega/Cinema Props, and Set Stuff for their antiquities so we could replicate the past. Finally to our models, whose images are forever captured in our vintage holidays, thank-you so very much.

Jeanne's heartfelt love, kisses, and thank-yous are for the two wonderful men in her life, John and Dylan, who provide endless support and a lot of silly fun.

Jim thanks his family, including Marylou, Jim, Erin, and Matt, as well as both Chris and Julie, for helping make today's celebrations both fun and meaningful.

Thank you,
Jim McCann and Jeanne Benedict

Introduction

Holidays are a living history of nostalgic moments spent with family and friends that forever capture the spirit of our celebrations. During these festive times we joyously feast, revel in folklore, and dust off treasured family heirlooms that warm our hearts. As we practice traditions sculpted by our ancestors years ago, many add our own artistry to enrich customs for modern times and growing families. In our book, we journey throughout the decades in hopes of bringing home holidays of the past to breathe new life into future celebrations.

Celebrations presents holidays depicted in different eras that either epitomize the occasion or helped to launch the observance into the fabric of society. Classic Victorian images of hearts and roses along with lower postal rates in 1890 prompted us to place Valentine's Day within this romantic time frame. The wholesome character of those living in 1950 led to trick-or-treaters collecting money for the needy, and this is why Halloween landed its broom midcentury. A cheerful stage has been set for a Renaissance Saint Patrick's Day with flowery maidens dancing and merry men knighted with shamrock talismans. Best of all, each of these holiday scenarios is accompanied by recipes organized into menus and decorating instructions, helping you to re-create the suggested occasions or fashion fabulous parties of your own invention.

The ideas offered in *Celebrations* blend traditional holiday food and decor while reflecting the era with a contemporary flair. We know you'll want to serve your grandmother's stuffing at Thanksgiving, but why not spice up the sweet potatoes with a little molasses and ginger? While your Christmas dinner may not be complete without the antique seasonal china, you can add some sparkle with costume jewelry as napkin adornments. We've shared tricks of the flower trade and secrets from catering pros, everything from lighting effects to napkin folds, to help make your preparations smooth and your event enjoyable.

In raising our glass to the past, we hope you will discover new holiday customs to call your own. Have fun, be happy, and celebrate!

A Victorian Valentine's Day

February 14, 1890

The Story of Valentine's Day

Saint Valentine, for whom this day is named, is said to be the patron saint of love, betrothed couples, beekeepers, epilepsy, happy marriages, plague, travelers, and young people, to name a few. It's no wonder that love can be full of turmoil when the head guy is also keeping bees and fighting the plague.

The celebration of Valentine's Day is loosely based on the Roman celebration of Lupercalia. This festival of eroticism honored the god Lupercus, who watched over shepherd's flocks, keeping them safe from wolves, and Juno Februata, a goddess of fertility and love. On February 15, young men and women would pull one another's names from an ancient hat and then spend the day feasting and often engaging in more than hand-holding. The Church in Rome, not fond of anyone holding anything in that manner, began replacing the names of the citizens with the names of

The first valentine is penned in the "pen" when the imprisoned Charles, Duke of Orleans, writes romantic verses for his wife to pass the time in 1415.

FEBRUARY
National Snack Food Month

Pay a Compliment Day (February 6)

Friendship Week (February 18 to 24)

saints. One had to "act out" the qualities of the saint that the church officials drew for the next year. The Church also changed the day to February 14 in A.D. 270 to distance itself from the concupiscent ides of February. This didn't fare well among the celebrants and a compromise had to be made. Less lust, more romance.

Saint Valentine was beheaded on February 14. He was a fair, you might even say chaste, guy, perfect to take on the lascivious behavior of the Lupercalia lovers. He lost his head by secretly marrying couples when Emperor Claudius II forbade it. The emperor felt that his subjects' hearts belonged to him and his war efforts and that love and marriage were a distraction. One legend tells us that while Saint Valentine was in prison awaiting his execution he fell in love with the jailer's daughter. In his parting letter to her he sealed the fate of the day by signing "From Your Valentine."

In memory of the martyr Saint Valentine we celebrate love. At some point, hearts and flowers were exchanged from lovers on the day because they were experiencing difficulties in their relationship. In the seventeenth century, England recognized Valentine's Day as a time to acknowledge loved ones. At the end of the nineteenth century, postage rates in United States dropped and the practice of sending Valentine's Day cards escalated. Today the U.S. Postal Service acts as a modern-day cupid, delivering love messages to millions every Valentine's Day.

Festive Traditions and Folklore

From notorious beginnings, the celebration of Saint Valentine's Day has come to symbolize love around the world. We chose to place our Valentine holiday in Victorian times (1837–1901) as the romantic artwork from this era epitomizes many of the images we see on Valentine's Day cards today. In fact, Victorian Valentine's Day cards are highly collectible, often garnering a high price at auction. Also cheaper postage rates of the era, such as the 1890 introduction of the "penny" postcard, contributed to an increase in the popularity and economic feasibility of sending a whimsical Valentine's Day greeting to a loved one.

Our most common Valentine's Day traditions include giving cards, red roses, chocolates, and a romantic dinner. It's the personal touches such as a handmade Valentine or an intimate feast lovingly prepared by a paramour that can capture one's heart. However, a dozen red roses truly say, "I love you." We invite you to create a Victorian Valentine's Day with traditions old and new to make it your very own.

Sending Valentine's Day Cards

Valentines have been around in some form or other since the fifteenth century. The holiday's love letters that we exchange today have origins in the eighteenth century as fancy paper designed with flowers and hearts. People wrote their own messages or they looked to a little book called the *Valentine Writer* for an inspirational verse.

From 1840 to 1860, Valentine's Day cards were works of art, often hand-painted and adorned with silk, lace, fresh flowers or sachets, glass ornamentation, and gold-leaf accents. Esther Howland is credited as the first person to sell and mass-produce these lavish valentines at a price that ranged from five to thirty dollars for one card. A pretty penny in the mid-1800s! The artistry became a little less detailed, but late-nineteenth-century cards were still decorated with items such as feathers, faux flowers, and costume jewelry.

What started as a handwritten note expressing "I love you" has turned into an amorous empire. Approximately one billion valentines are sent each year on this day of love. Electronic valentines are also sent to friends and loved ones with romantic music, dancing hearts, and even recording capabilities so you can utter sweet nothings to your recipient over the World Wide Web. A great timesaver for those on the go, but the Internet is perhaps a touch impersonal for your sweetheart.

Red Roses to the One I Love

Roses have long been known as the "flower of love" as mythology proclaims them to be the favorite of Venus, Roman goddess of love. The red rose symbolizes love and passion, and the gift of a dozen red roses to your valentine is customary on this day. Yellow roses signify friendship and

In 1847, the United States Post Office introduces adhesive stamps, which simplify post office operations along with everyone's mailing labors.

A lucky thirty-five million people receive heart-shaped boxes of chocolate in the year 2000.

white roses purity and faith. The pink rose means happiness, which presents an ironic twist for this holiday, because a pink almond tree blossomed over Saint Valentine's grave.

Red Hearts

An obvious symbol of love, as the heart is considered to be the seat of emotion. The heart beats fast when one is excited or filled with the idea of a lover. Some people may be ruled by their hearts, but others happily open them up, especially on Valentine's Day.

A Heart-Shaped Box of Chocolates

Chocolate has long been associated with this holiday, as it is allegedly a natural aphrodisiac. Phenylethylamine, a substance found in chocolate, is supposed to make people feel as if they are falling in love. Packaging chocolates in a heart-shaped red box for Valentine's Day was the brilliant marketing idea of chocolatiers.

Candy Conversation Hearts

These tiny heart-shaped candies with an embossed message have been around since 1902! A favorite of children to exchange in school with racy sayings like "Be Mine," the manufacturer, Necco, currently sells about eight billion of these confectionary gems on Valentine's Day.

That Rosy-Cheeked Cupid

A popular little angel on Valentine's Day, this mythological cherub flew around shooting arrows into one's heart. According to legend, people struck would not perish but live to fall in love with the first person they saw.

In 1929, the infamous Saint Valentine's Day Massacre takes place in Chicago. Al Capone's henchmen, posing as police officers, shoot down seven members of rival gangster George Moran's crew.

Valentine's Day Rendezvous for Two

Victorian-era cuisine was both lavish and elegant, which inspired us to design this decadent Valentine's Day menu. For our 1890 rendezvous, aphrodisiac foods blended with some edible tidbits reminiscent of olden days promise the perfect romantic interlude. Dinner parties were a common practice among late-nineteenth-century bon vivants with menus offering twelve or more courses at one sitting. Oysters were a popular starter followed by consommé, poached fish, beef fillet, game fowl, and endless toppings of rich, creamy sauces.

For Valentine's Day, aphrodisiac foods are a must. Artichokes were popularized by Catherine dé Médicis, wed at fourteen years of age, whose passion for the sensuous greens were said to be notorious. Other classic "love" foods include seeds and nuts known for the potency they derive from ample amounts of zinc, and asparagus for its masculine form. Coincidentally many of these foods are found in Victorian cuisine. People of the time took pleasure in indulgence and luxury. What a perfect way to celebrate Valentine's Day.

Port Wine–Glazed Quail on Currant Pancakes

Chicken, Artichoke, and Pistachio Paupiettes with Citrus and Yellow Tomato Coulis

Asparagus with Light Raspberry Sauce

Chocolate Espresso Mousse

Chardonnay or Mineral Water

Port Wine–Glazed Quail on Currant Pancakes

This delicate dish is an ideal way to start your meal. However, for a time-saver, you can substitute prepared dollar-size pancakes found in the frozen food section of the grocery store. Warm the pancakes in the microwave and serve with the quail.

2 (6-ounce) quail	½ medium-sized red onion, finely slivered
¼ teaspoon salt	1 cup ruby port
¼ teaspoon ground black pepper	1 tablespoon butter
2 tablespoons olive oil	Currant Pancakes (see recipe below)

MAKES 2 APPETIZER SERVINGS

Using a sharp knife or poultry shears, cut out the backbone and pluck the tiny rib bones from each quail and discard. Open quail up and press down on breastbone to flatten. Rinse quail and pat dry. Season both sides with salt and pepper.

Heat the oil in a large skillet over medium-high heat. Place the quail, breast side down, in pan. Cook until quail is browned, 2 to 3 minutes. Using tongs, turn quail over and add onion and port to skillet. Cook until quail reaches desired doneness, 5 to 8 minutes. Remove the quail from skillet to a plate and cover to keep warm. Increase heat to high and cook until liquid reduces to half, about 1 minute.

Arrange 3 Currant Pancakes on each of 2 plates. Place 1 quail on pancakes, on each plate. Remove skillet from heat and swirl butter into reduced port. Drizzle port sauce over quail and serve immediately.

Currant Pancakes

Use butter sparingly to grease the skillet as generous amounts may make the pancakes soggy.

¾ cup all-purpose flour	⅔ cup milk
½ teaspoon baking powder	1 egg, lightly beaten
⅛ teaspoon baking soda	½ teaspoon freshly grated lemon zest
Pinch salt	Butter, for cooking
1 teaspoon sugar	¼ cup dried zante currants

MAKES ABOUT 14 DOLLAR-SIZE PANCAKES

Sift together the flour, baking powder, baking soda, salt, and sugar in a bowl until combined. Make a well in the center of the flour mixture. Add the milk, egg, and zest to the well and stir until combined. Cover with plastic wrap and let stand 15 minutes.

Add ½ teaspoon butter to a skillet over medium heat. For each pancake, spoon 1 tablespoon of the batter into skillet, forming a pancake about 2 inches in diameter. Sprinkle 1 teaspoon of the currants over each pancake. Cook until top is bubbling, about 1 minute; flip over with a spatula. Cook until underside is light brown, about 1 minute, and remove from skillet with spatula. Continue with remaining batter, adding small amounts of butter to the skillet as needed. Serve warm. (Store extra pancakes, covered in plastic wrap, in the refrigerator up to 2 days.)

Chicken, Artichoke, and Pistachio Paupiettes with Citrus and Yellow Tomato Coulis

A lovely presentation, these chicken breasts are stuffed with a blend of exotic ingredients that are sure to tantalize your sweetheart's palate.

4 boneless, skinless chicken breast halves, fat trimmed	CITRUS AND YELLOW TOMATO COULIS
	1 tablespoon butter
2 tablespoons olive oil	1 tablespoon olive oil
½ teaspoon salt	⅓ cup minced leek, white part only
¼ teaspoon pepper	¼ cup brandy
1 cup canned water packed artichoke hearts, drained, finely chopped	1 cup chicken broth
1 clove garlic, minced	3 cups yellow baby teardrop tomatoes, coarsely chopped
½ cup freshly grated Parmesan cheese	¼ cup fresh orange juice
1 cup cooked instant couscous, unseasoned	1 tablespoon fresh lemon juice
½ cup ground pistachio nuts	⅛ teaspoon salt
1 tablespoon fresh lemon juice	Pinch white pepper

MAKES 2 TO 4 SERVINGS

Soak 12 wooden picks in water 30 minutes. Preheat oven to 350F (175C). Grease a baking sheet with 1 tablespoon of the olive oil.

Pound chicken breasts with a kitchen mallet to ¼-inch thickness. Rub remaining 1 tablespoon olive oil, salt, and pepper on chicken breasts.

Mix together artichokes, garlic, Parmesan cheese, couscous, pistachios, and lemon juice until combined.

Mound ½ cup of the artichoke mixture along center on underside of chicken breast. Wrap breast around mixture by pulling edges from long sides of breast up over mixture. Overlap edges of breast on top of mixture and insert a wooden pick to secure edges closed. Place chicken, wooden pick side down, on prepared baking sheet.

Bake for 40 minutes, or until chicken center is no longer pink.

Meanwhile, to make the coulis: Heat butter and oil in a skillet over medium-high heat. Add leek and cook until tender, 3 to 5 minutes. Increase heat to high and add brandy. Cook until liquid is reduced by half, about 1 minute. Add chicken broth, tomatoes, orange juice, and lemon juice and stir to combine. Reduce the heat to low and simmer, uncovered, for 30 minutes.

Remove from heat and pour mixture into a food processor. Process until smooth. Pour mixture through a sieve into a medium bowl and stir in salt and white pepper. Makes about 2 cups

Arrange chicken on a platter. Pour a little of the coulis over chicken and serve remaining coulis on the side. (Store coulis covered in plastic wrap for up to 2 days in the refrigerator.)

Asparagus with Light Raspberry Sauce

Try this tangy raspberry sauce as a dressing on a green salad as well.

1 pound asparagus spears, washed	3 tablespoons fresh lemon juice
1 cup fresh raspberries	¼ teaspoon salt
¼ cup olive oil	⅛ teaspoon white pepper

MAKES 2 TO 4 SERVINGS

VARIATION To match photo on page 5, arrange Chicken, Artichoke, and Pistachio Paupiettes with Citrus and Yellow Tomato Coulis (page 7) in center of a large serving plate. Arrange asparagus in a heart shape around edge of plate. Puree frozen raspberries and strain out seeds. Spoon puree in space between chicken and asparagus. Sprinkle a few raspberries over asparagus and top chicken with hearts cut from fruit or pastry.

Preheat oven to 450F (205C). Trim about ½ inch off bottom ends of asparagus spears and place in a 13 × 9-inch baking dish.

Using the back of a spoon, force raspberries through a sieve over a bowl to strain juice from seeds. Add oil, lemon juice, salt, and pepper to raspberry juice and whisk until combined. Pour mixture over asparagus spears and turn spears to coat.

Bake 8 to 10 minutes, or until spears are roasted. Remove from heat and arrange on a platter. Pour the sauce over asparagus and serve warm.

Chocolate Espresso Mousse

This classic dessert is a lovely way to end a meal and a sweet way to begin a romantic interlude.

3 ounces unsweetened baking chocolate, chopped

5 tablespoons sugar

2 eggs, pasteurized

½ cup heavy cream

½ teaspoon instant espresso powder

1 tablespoon Kahlúa

MAKES 2 TO 4 SERVINGS

Melt chocolate over medium-low heat in top of double boiler, stirring constantly. Cool 8 minutes. Beat sugar and eggs in a medium bowl until mixture thickens and is pale yellow. Beat in melted chocolate until incorporated. Add cream and beat until cream thickens. Dissolve espresso powder in Kahlúa and stir into mixture until blended. Pour chocolate mixture into 2 to 4 stemmed glasses. Refrigerate uncovered until chocolate mousse sets, about 3 hours.

Place glasses on individual plates and serve cool. (Store covered in plastic wrap for up to 4 days.)

Valentine's Day Decor and Personal Touches

Velvet flower appliqués on a sheer overlay, and ribbon and charm-tied napkins set a romantic table.

Velvet Flower Appliqués on Sheer Overlay for Table

FROM FABRIC STORE: 60 inches of 60-inch-wide pink organza; ½ yard each of 3 to 4 different colored velvets, including green; 7 yards of pink fringe; fabric glue

Using fabric glue, adhere fringe to perimeter of organza square. Cut out flower shapes from velvets other than green. Cut out leaves from green velvet. Spread a thin layer of fabric glue on back of velvet shapes and around outer edges to keep velvet from fraying. Adhere shapes to organza, creating a floral border or an all-over floral design.

NOTES ON FABRIC: This overlay is recommended for a round table with a diameter of less than 40 inches or a similar-size square table. Fabric is usually made in 45-inch or 60-inch widths and cut to whatever length you request.

A Charming Place Setting

Dangle a locket with a picture of your sweetheart or a little love message inside by wrapping the locket's chain around the neck of a decanter or bottle of wine. Purchase jewelry charms with a Victorian or love motif. Feed ribbon (1-foot length) through the metal loop on a charm and tie ribbon around a rolled napkin or the stem of a glass.

Hand-Tied Rose Bouquet

FROM FLORIST: 5 pink roses; 8 red roses; 12 Galax leaves

FROM CRAFT STORE: 1 (12-inch length, 22-gauge) green floral wire; 2 yards sheer pink ribbon

Cut rose stems to 12-inch lengths and strip stems of thorns. Remove leaves from bottom half of stems. Build bouquet from center starting with pink roses in a bunch. Add a collar of red roses around pink roses and wrap green floral wire around upper middle of stems to bind. Insert Galax stems into floral wire around red roses. Wrap pink ribbon around gathered stems covering floral wire and tie off with a bow.

Roses are hand-tied into a bouquet for your valentine.

Renaissance Revelry for Saint Patrick's Day

March 17, 1600

The Story of Saint Patrick's Day

Ireland's patron saint, Patrick (A.D. 385–461) was a real man of legendary proportions. Much of what we know of him is myth. However, through his writings, the *Confessio* in particular, we come to learn that from a tragic childhood he rose to be one of the most celebrated people on the planet. The *Confessio,* written in Latin around A.D. 450, is basically an auto-biography and self-deprecating confession of how Patrick was kidnapped at age sixteen, an act that he attributes to his lack of faith in God. He was then sold into slavery, from which he eventually escaped. Patrick wanted to share with all how he found the power to pick himself up by his boot-straps and overcome his fear of men criticizing him for a lack of education. A burning spirit fueled by a prophetic dream brought him back to the Emerald Isle in A.D. 432 as a missionary.

Ordained as a priest and then as a bishop, Saint Patrick is widely

The luck of the Irish is with George Washington in 1776 when the British evacuate Boston on Saint Patrick's Day, leaving the Americans to take over the city.

MARCH
National Play the Recorder Month

National Procrastinator's Week (second week of March)

Panic Day (March 9)

Proud Irish men and women shed a green tear when President Truman becomes the first president to attend the New York City Saint Paddy's Day Parade in 1948.

In 1995, the Irish government finally decides to celebrate Saint Patrick's Day with beer, fun, and frolic. The world's largest Saint Patrick's Day celebration is launched in Ireland, better late than never.

accepted as one of the first to bring Christianity to Ireland. The famous tale of Saint Patrick driving the snakes out of Ireland is considered to be an allegorical rendering of his conversion of pagans to Christianity. Historians suggest that the snakes represent serpents or evil, which many relate to the paganism of the time. However, the fable goes that Saint Patrick stood on a hill with a wooden staff, which he used to drive the snakes into the sea and forever away from the isle.

As he was a well-traveled and wise man who preached the gospel throughout numerous countries, many knew and loved him. It is believed that Saint Patrick died around A.D. 461 on March 17, which is why we honor his memory on this date. Saint Patrick's creative use of the shamrock as a visual representation of the Trinity during sermons has made the wee clover famous. The shamrock, appearing in everything from shaped cookies to emblems on flags, is the holiday's main symbol. The first American observance of Saint Patrick's Day on record was in 1737 in Boston, Massachusetts. Today most major cities host a big parade, with the events at the New York and Chicago pageants making national news headlines. A joyous celebration that exalts a wonderful man, this day is full of so much merriment it has all seeing green!

Festive Traditions and Folklore

The Renaissance period, rich in revelry, is ripe for a Saint Paddy's Day celebration. Many towns have a Renaissance with ladies in lace-up corsets and flower halos and lords sporting tights and not much else. We don't expect the guys to go pubhopping in panty hose, but we do hope all will have a festive time of feasting as they did in the days of Shakespeare.

Trippingly off the tongue come the many blessings and phrases of all who are "Irish for the day." Known for their gift of gab, over the years the Irish have corralled the masses to join in with the Saint Patrick's Day celebrations. Everyone must wear green or they are prey for pinchers. "Kiss me I'm Irish" is proposed with the usual response of "Would you like a green breath mint?" "Erin Go Braugh," meaning "Ireland Forever," are the toasting words of friends who gather to dance jigs and sing old Irish tunes. May the luck of the Irish be yours on this the happiest of holidays.

Shamrocks, Shamrocks Everywhere!

As the Emerald Isle introduced this holiday it is only fitting that it be tied to any and everything green. However, the green of Saint Patrick's Day has many associations. The shamrock, used by Saint Patrick to symbolize the Trinity, is the most common connection. Green is also a sign of spring and renewal. This meaning is twofold in that the holiday takes place on the vernal March 17 and honors a man who brought new religious ideas to a nation. Some say green symbolizes an ancient Irish practice in which farmers burned green leaves in spring. The ashes were spread over the fields to make the soil more fertile. Wearing mulch on Saint Pat's Day would be an unpleasant tradition, so we wear green.

Pinch Me Till I Turn Green

Although it is a popular custom to pinch those not wearing green on Saint Patrick's Day, it is not an Irish tradition. We have American schoolchildren to thank for the ritualistic and painful tweaking of the greenless on March 17.

Leprechauns

This little Irish fairy has come to be a Saint Patrick's Day figure as well as a cereal-box pinup boy. According to legend, the breakfast icon is much friendlier than the elf. Leprechauns wear tiny green top hats and masquerade as shoemakers (why would anyone with a pot of gold work for a living?). The trick to catching a leprechaun is to listen for the tinkering of his wee cobbler's hammer. If caught, he must tell you where his pot of gold is, typically at a rainbow's end. But be wary, as he'll trick ya and you'll never win the lottery, but take heart: You may find a prize in a box of Lucky Charms cereal.

Jumping on the Irish-folklore bandwagon, General Mills launches Lucky Charms cereal in 1964. Post-baby boomers everywhere recall Saturday cartoons ads boasting the "magically delicious" powers of pink hearts, yellow moons, orange stars, and green clovers made from marshmallow.

Saint Patrick's Day Parades

Ireland gave birth to this holiday, but the first Saint Patrick's Day parade was held in New York City on March 17, 1762. Irishmen, soldiers serving in the English army, marched down the street to the music of their homeland. As more Irish emigrated to the United States; Saint Patrick's Day parades became a way to show the unity of their heritage and feel a sense of home in a foreign land. Chicago's parade, which originated on March 17, 1843, is made more festive by the addition of forty pounds of green dye to the Chicago River. Dye had been used to detect waste in the river, and in 1962, a labor leader turned sanitation into celebration and the traditional green river on Saint Patrick's Day was born.

The Shamrock Shake is introduced in Ireland's McDonald's in the 1980s. These green-colored milkshakes quickly make their way to United States and become a favorite around Saint Patrick's Day.

In 1998, England's John Evans balances eleven empty beer kegs on his head for ten seconds, winning the beer-keg-balancing title in the *Guinness Book of World Records*.

Saint Paddy's Supper for Eight

A Saint Patrick's Day celebration isn't complete without corned beef, cabbage, and of course, potatoes. And then there's the green hue that pops up in everything from bread to beer. Ironically, corned beef and cabbage was not popular on Irish menus of yore. Pork was the entrée on most Irish tables, as cows were highly valued for their milk.

Corned beef, named for the corn-size salt grains used in old preserving methods, was considered a delicacy, according to late fifth-century literature, as salt was expensive. We've put a trendy twist on the traditional corned-beef-and-cabbage recipe that became popular in America as Saint Paddy's Day fare. Much of the other foods such as Apple Mash, and Irish Tea Bread are as old as the Blarney Stone, making them perfect for a celebration set in the 1600s. Colcannon, a cabbage-and-potato side dish, is also a Saint Pat's classic, but we thought cabbage in one dish would give all their fill of green.

Corned Beef Cabbage Rolls
with Mustard Cider Sauce

Gingersnap Lamb Stew

Apple Mash

Irish Tea Bread

Irish Stout or Apple Cider

Corned Beef Cabbage Rolls with Mustard Cider Sauce

These cabbage rolls are a wee bit labor-intensive, but absolutely delicious. The mustard cider sauce adds a nice sweetness, but you can also serve these rolls topped with the juices from the baking dish.

1 tablespoon mustard seeds

½ tablespoon peppercorns

1 tablespoon coriander seeds

½ tablespoon whole allspice

2 bay leaves

1 tablespoon vegetable oil

1 tablespoon butter

1 clove garlic, minced

1 cup finely chopped onion

1 cup finely chopped carrot

1 (2-pound) corned beef brisket

½ cup white wine vinegar

6 ounces Guinness stout

½ teaspoon salt

2 cups shredded green cabbage

2 pounds russet potatoes, peeled, cut into 1-inch cubes

1 (2- to 3-pound) green cabbage head

MUSTARD CIDER SAUCE
½ cup apple cider

1 tablespoon whole-grain brown mustard

1 cup heavy cream

MAKES ABOUT 18 ROLLS

Make a bouquet garni by placing mustard seeds, peppercorns, coriander, allspice, and bay leaves in a cheesecloth bag and tie to close.

Add oil and butter to a large nonreactive stockpot over medium-high heat. Add garlic, onion, and carrot and cook until tender, about 8 minutes. Add corned beef, vinegar, stout, salt, and bouquet garni. Add enough water to pot so that water just covers beef. Cover and bring to a boil over high heat. Reduce heat to medium-low and simmer until beef is tender and shreds easily with a fork, about 3 hours.

Add shredded cabbage and potatoes to pot with beef. Cover and simmer until potatoes are tender, 15 to 20 minutes.

Meanwhile, remove the center core from head of cabbage using a sharp knife. Place cabbage in a large stockpot and cover with water. Cook until outer leaves are bright green and tender, 2 to 3 minutes. Lift cabbage from water and remove outer leaves. Return cabbage to boiling water and repeat process of cooking and removing outer leaves until all leaves are cooked. Trim thick center vein from bottom of each leaf. Reserve 4 large outer leaves to line baking dish. Set aside.

Using tongs, remove beef to a cutting board. Remove bouquet garni and discard. Pour liquid and vegetables in pot through a colander over a large bowl. Reserve liquid. Transfer vegetables into another large bowl. Mash vegetables until potatoes are smooth and vegetables are evenly distributed throughout mixture.

Cut off fat from beef and discard. Finely mince meat and stir into potato mixture.

To make cabbage rolls, spread about 1/3 cup beef-potato mixture over center of each cabbage leaf. Fold sides of cabbage leaf over filling and, starting with the stem end, roll up cabbage.

Preheat oven to 325F (165C). Line a 13 × 9-inch glass baking dish with reserved outside leaves. Neatly arrange cabbage rolls on leaves in dish. Pour reserved liquid from corned beef over rolls in dish. Cover with foil and cook 40 minutes until cabbage rolls shrink slightly.

To make mustard cider sauce: Combine cider and mustard in a small saucepan over medium-high heat. Cook, stirring occasionally, until mixture reduces by half. Reduce heat to low and add cream. Cook, stirring occasionally, until cream thickens, about 10 minutes. Remove from heat and transfer to a small serving bowl. Makes about 1 cup.

Using tongs, remove cabbage rolls from baking dish and arrange on serving platter. Drizzle a little mustard cider sauce over top and serve remaining sauce on side.

Gingersnap Lamb Stew

Gingersnap cookies are used as a thickening ingredient and to add zip to this traditional Saint Paddy's Day favorite.

2 tablespoons vegetable oil	2 tablespoons chopped fresh parsley
2 cloves garlic, minced	1 teaspoon fresh thyme leaves
3 pounds lamb stew meat, cut in 1-inch chunks	1/2 teaspoon salt
	1/2 teaspoon black pepper
4 large carrots, peeled, cut in chunks	4 cups beef broth
2 onions, cut in slivers	3 cups water
4 russet potatoes, scrubbed, cut in 1-inch chunks	10 crushed gingersnap cookies
1 cup frozen green peas	8 small round bread loaves (optional)

MAKES 8 SERVINGS

Heat oil and garlic in a large stockpot over medium-high heat. Add lamb and cook, turning frequently, until browned on all sides. Add remaining ingredients to pot and bring to a boil. Reduce heat to low and cover. Cook, stirring occasionally, until lamb is done and vegetables are tender, 2 hours.

Serve in hollowed-out round loaves of bread or in individual bowls.

Irish Tea Bread

Also called "barm brack," this bread or a variation is enjoyed on Saint Patrick's Day and on Halloween in Ireland. This version, similar to a nut quick bread, is made with dried fruit soaked in tea.

1 1/2 cups brewed black tea, cold	3/4 cup packed light brown sugar
1/2 cup golden raisins	1/4 cup butter, melted
1/2 cup dark raisins	1 1/2 cups all-purpose flour
1/4 cup dried zante currants	1 teaspoon baking powder
2 eggs, lightly beaten	

MAKES 8 TO 12 SERVINGS

Place tea, raisins, and currants in a bowl. Cover and soak at least 3 hours or overnight. Drain tea from fruit and reserve 1/2 cup of tea.

Preheat oven to 350F (175C). Butter and flour an 8-inch round pan.

Beat eggs and sugar in a large bowl until fluffy. Add butter and reserved 1/2 cup tea and mix well. Sift together flour and baking powder and beat into mixture until just combined. Stir in fruit until evenly distributed throughout. Pour batter into prepared pan. Bake for 40 minutes or until wooden pick inserted into bread comes out clean.

Cool in pan for 5 minutes and turn out onto a wire rack to completely cool or serve warm. Transfer to serving platter and cut into wedges.

Apple Mash

Odd, we know, but the combination of golden potatoes and apples in this old Irish side dish is exquisite. Use any leftovers to make potato pancakes the next morning.

4 pounds (about 8 medium) Yukon Gold potatoes, peeled, cut into 1-inch cubes

1 tablespoon salt

1½ pounds (about 2 large) Red Delicious apples, peeled, diced

2 tablespoons water

2 tablespoons sugar

5 tablespoons butter, softened

MAKES 8 SERVINGS

Add potatoes and salt to a stockpot and cover with water. Bring water to a boil over medium-high heat and cook until potatoes are tender, 15 to 20 minutes. Drain potatoes in a colander.

Meanwhile, place apples, water, and sugar in a large saucepan over medium-high heat. Cook, stirring occasionally, until apples are tender, about 10 minutes.

Transfer potatoes to a large bowl and mash until smooth. Add apples and butter and beat until combined.

Spoon into large bowl and serve warm. (Store in an airtight container in the refrigerator for up to 2 days.)

St. Patrick's Day Decor and Personal Touches

Flower Head Wreath for Ladies

For each wreath, buy the following:

FROM FLORIST: 2 Caspia stems, 6 purple daisies, assorted spring flowers

FROM CRAFT STORE: 1 roll 22-gauge, green floral wire; 5 different colors thin cloth ribbons in 2-foot lengths

Lay Caspia stems on a flat surface in a 2-foot-long line. Using wire cutters, cut 15 to 20 (2½-inch-long) pieces of floral wire. Wrap wire pieces around Caspia stems to attach them to each other. Form attached stems into a wreath and secure wreath by wrapping with wire pieces. Make sure wire ends are safe by bending ends into wreath.

To prepare daisies, trim stems to 1-inch lengths. Insert a wire piece into the bottom of a daisy stem and slide up through the top bloom of the flower. The wire should extend ¾ inch above the top bloom. Bend ¾ inch of wire into a crook or small hook. Gently pull wire down from bottom of daisy stem so crook inserts back into top bloom. Arrange daisies on wreath and secure by bending the daisies' wire stems around Caspia stems. To prepare spring flowers, trim stems to 1-inch lengths. Insert wire pieces horizontally through calyx (seed box) of each flower below bloom. Bend wire down into hairpin shape and twist wire ends together like a corkscrew. Arrange flowers around wreath and bend wire around Caspia stems to secure. Gather ribbons and tie to back of wreath, finishing with a bow.

A fresh flower wreath adds an Irish country touch.

Shamrock Talisman Necklaces

For 4 necklaces, buy the following:

FROM CRAFT STORE: 1 (2-ounce) pack emerald green or green pearlized Sculpey III modeling clay, shamrock cookie cutter, 4 yards brown suede string, 16 decorative beads

Condition the clay by stretching and twisting it for about 3 minutes until smooth and pliable. Using a glass bottle, roll out clay on a flat surface to 1/16-inch thickness. Cut out shamrock shapes using cookie cutters. Using a skewer, poke a hole 1/4 inch in from top edge of shamrock. Line a baking sheet with aluminum foil and place shamrocks on foil. FOLLOW MANUFACTURER'S INSTRUCTIONS FOR BAKING CLAY IN YOUR OVEN IN A WELL-VENTILATED AREA. According to manufacturer's instructions, clay is usually baked at 275F (130C) for 20 minutes. Do not microwave! Cool clay completely. Feed suede string through hole in top of shamrock and string beads on either side to decorate. Knot ends of string to desired length for guests to wear as necklaces or to hang on steins or mugs (photo on page 12).

Renaissance Costumes

Inquire about costume rental at a costume shop, high school or college theater department, or community theater. Often they have a wardrobe collection used for Shakespearean plays placed in the late sixteenth and early seventeenth centuries. Pass on the information to your guests so they may all come in Renaissance dress.

A Modern Passover in the Year 5761

April 2001

The Story of Passover

No matter what religion or culture we come from, most know the biblical story of Moses and the Exodus from Egypt, where the Jewish people were enslaved under a harsh pharaoh. A seer told the pharaoh that a male baby would be born who would deliver the Jewish people from slavery. Upon hearing this, the pharaoh ordered that all Jewish male infants be killed. One mother put her endangered babe in a basket and set him afloat on the river in an effort to save his life. Baby Moses was found by the pharaoh's daughter and taken into the family.

When Moses became a man he learned of his Jewish heritage. One day he spied an Egyptian beating a Jewish slave and in defense of his brethren killed the Egyptian. Fearing for his life, Moses fled into the desert. While he was wandering in the desert, God appeared to him as a burning bush with a message that Moses was to go and free the Jewish people.

Moses bade the pharaoh to let his people go, but the ruler refused. Ten horrible plagues were sent down to Egypt from God. Frogs fell from the skies and swarms of locusts covered the land, but still the pharaoh refused to take heed. The tenth plague was that all the firstborn sons were to be slain. The Jewish people, who had been forewarned of this last plague, protected their sons by smearing lamb's blood over their doorways. When the Angel of Death saw the blood, it "passed over" their home and the lives were spared, but the Egyptians lost their sons.

Finally, the pharaoh freed the slaves and allowed the Jewish people to leave. Without a moment to spare, they packed up their homes and headed into the desert. The pharaoh reversed his decision and sent an army after them. The Jewish people were at the banks of the Red Sea when they saw the Egyptian troops. Moses miraculously parted the sea for his people to cross over to safety. When the Egyptians attempted to follow, the sea swallowed them up. Passover takes its name from a spiritual act of salvation, which led to the physical freedom of the Jewish people.

Festive Traditions and Folklore

The year 5761 on the Hebrew calendar falls between the years 2000/2001 on the Gregorian calendar. We have decided to set this holiday in modern times to highlight the timeless devotion of the Jewish people, who still practice the same traditions set forth thousands of years ago. Passover or Pesach is an eight-day-long observance in remembrance of the Jewish people's struggle and emancipation from slavery in Egypt.

The Seder, held on the first two nights of Passover, is a beautiful ritual during which families read the *Haggadah,* which tells the story of the exodus from Egypt and explains the seder rituals, and feast with symbolic food and wine. The word *seder,* translating as "detail" or "order" in Hebrew, is a celebration with deep meaning that both teaches and reminds us of the story of the flight from Egypt. The Seder ceremony involves the youngest child asking four questions as posed from the *Haggadah.* The answers not only explain why the acts of the evening are important but the history behind them as well. Passover is considered to be the most widely observed holiday of the Jewish people. We give you these time-honored traditions, with a few modern twists that some of our friends have incorporated into their Pesach celebration.

Significance of Matzo

During Passover, the consumption of food containing leavening ingredients is forbidden, and matzo, a flat, unleavened cracker, is usually substituted. This symbolic act recalls that when the Jewish people made their exodus from Egypt there was no time to let their bread rise. They brought their bread dough with them and baked it in the hot sun resulting in matzo. In preparation for the holiday, some people remove from their home all items that are *hametz,* such as yeast, baking powder, baking soda, or any food products that contain leavening ingredients, while others simply put them aside. On the night before the holiday, some people search through the house with a candle or flashlight to make sure their home is hametz-free. Some even use a feather to sweep away crumbs from any bread found. If anything is collected it must be burned in the morning. This practice is called *bedikat hametz,* which means "the search for leaven." Many also prepare by dusting off special silverware and dinnerware for the Seder.

The Seder Plate

A ceremonial plate, this symbol of the Jewish people's quest for freedom is the centerpiece of every Seder table. This traditional plate contains five items representative of the people's plight:

1. *Haroset* is a mixture usually of nuts, apples, honey, cinnamon, and wine signifying the mortar and bricks made by the Jewish slaves.

2. Parsley dipped in salt water is for the tears of the slaves.

washed thoroughly before being used.
RUBBER GLOVES: Might have a powder dusting.
PLAY-DOH: Could contain hametz, and therefore is not kosher for Passover.
ANT AND ROACH TRAPS: You got it . . . hametz. To keep bugs away during the holiday, use insecticide sprays.
CAT FOOD, DOG FOOD, AND FISH FOOD: Check the labels for a hametz-free pooch and kitty.
ELMER'S GLUE is acceptable for Passover use, but Elmer's Paste is not.

3. A roasted egg is a symbol for spring and some believe an offering to God.

4. A shank bone, usually a roasted lamb bone, or sometimes a turkey leg, symbolizes the sacrificial lamb whose blood was smeared over the doorways.

5. Bitter herbs of grated horseradish or lettuce are for the bitterness of the enslaved.

A Cup of Wine for Elijah

A goblet of wine is filled and placed on the table for Elijah. The door is also opened for this biblical prophet should he return announcing that the world will finally be at peace.

The *Haggadah*

The *Haggadah,* which translates to "telling" in Hebrew, is the book read at the Seder that outlines the ceremony and tells the story of Passover. Today, many of our friends have creative ways of carrying on this tradition including acting out the *Haggadah* as a play or even illustrating and rewording the story as a nursery rhyme. We think this to be a marvelous thing, because the youngest child questions everything!

"Why is this night different from all other nights?" is asked near the beginning of the ceremony, followed by an evening of more questions and the history of Passover. Celebrants dip the items on the Seder plate into other foods as they explain their meaning. All lean back in their chairs to relax and remember their freedom from enslavement.

The Afikomen

Early in the Seder, three matzos are placed in a cloth sleeve or matzo cover with three separate pockets. The matzo in the middle pocket is removed and broken in half. One half goes back into the pocket and the other half is wrapped up in a cloth and hidden. Some say this tradition is to keep the children intrigued during the Seder, wondering where the cracker could be. At the end of the meal the children hunt for the Afikomen and the one who finds it wins a prize. Many families will hide as many matzo pieces as there are children to keep all the little ones happy!

Passover Seder for Ten

The customs regarding the food that one may eat at the Passover Seder are deeply rooted in Jewish history and religion. This modern menu offers some new ideas for a Seder meal with foods that are acceptable for the occasion, but always check to see that the ingredients are labeled "kosher for Passover."

Most of the Jewish population in America is Ashkenazi, coming from Russia, and Germany. At the Ashkenazic Passover the use of food containing leavening ingredients is forbidden (see significance of Matzo page 27). Legumes and grains are also not allowed because they swell when mixed with water. The Sephardic Jews, with roots in the Mediterranean region, Asia, and parts of the Middle East, allow grains and rice in their Seder dishes, but also refrain from leavened items. Matzo, is usually substituted in various forms for bread products along with potato starch for thickening.

Why the cultural and culinary distinction? Some Ashkenazi Jews will "go Sephardic" occasionally for their Passover celebration to expand their food options while remaining somewhat traditional.

Salmon Gefilte Fish

Homemade Chicken Soup
with Herbed Matzo Balls

Orange Brisket with
Carrot-Onion Stuffing

Sautéed fresh spinach
with shallots

Kosher wine

Mandelbrot Pear and
Cashew Crisp

Salmon Gefilte Fish

Gefilte is derived from the Yiddish language and means "stuffed fish." Originally a fish mixture was stuffed into the fish skin and cooked. Gefilte fish is usually made from a combination of whitefish, pike, and carp. However, this Passover starter made with salmon in a light broth is still acceptable Seder fare.

FISH BROTH

1 1/2 pounds salmon fish bones

8 cups water

1 large fennel bulb, coarsely chopped

2 carrots, peeled, cut into 1-inch chunks

3 tablespoons chopped fresh parsley

1 tablespoon salt

1 teaspoon white pepper

SALMON GEFILTE FISH

2 tablespoons vegetable oil

1 cup minced fennel bulb (reserve green sprigs for garnish)

2 pounds salmon fillet, skinned

1 tablespoon minced fresh parsley

2 eggs, lightly beaten

1/3 cup matzo meal

3 tablespoons water

2 teaspoons fresh lemon juice

1 teaspoon salt

1/2 teaspoon white pepper

1/2 teaspoon sugar

MAKES 10 SERVINGS

To make the broth: Rinse bones thoroughly and put into large stockpot. Add remaining ingredients to pot and bring to a boil over medium-high heat. Reduce heat to low, cover, and simmer for 30 minutes. Remove from heat and cool, covered, for at least 1 hour. Pour fish broth through a sieve over a large bowl. Make sure all fish bones have been strained from broth. Pour broth back into pot. Cover and set aside. Discard solids.

To make the Salmon Gefilte Fish: Heat oil in a large skillet over medium-high heat. Add fennel and cook, stirring occasionally, until tender, 5 to 8 minutes.

Cut salmon fillet into small chunks and add in batches to a food processor. Process each batch until just pureed, 5 to 10 seconds. Transfer salmon puree to a large bowl.

Add fennel and parsley to salmon and stir to incorporate. Add eggs, matzo meal, water, lemon juice, salt, white pepper, and sugar and stir until combined. Cover with plastic wrap and chill for 30 minutes.

Bring fish broth to a boil over medium-high heat. With moistened hands, shape fish mixture into ovals, using 2 tablespoons dough per oval. Using a long-handled spoon carefully lower ovals into boiling broth as they are shaped. Reduce heat to medium. Cover and cook 30 minutes, gently turning ovals after 15 minutes. When ovals rise to surface of broth fish will be done. Keep partially covered, and cool completely. Cover and refrigerate overnight.

Arrange 2 to 3 gefilte fish pieces on each individual serving plate and spoon a small amount of broth over each. Garnish with green sprigs from fennel. Serve cool.

Homemade Chicken Soup with Herbed Matzo Balls

Chicken soup, with its fabled powers, has been labeled as a cure-all for everything from the common cold to the restless soul.

4 pounds chicken fryer parts (wings, thighs, drumsticks)

4 quarts (16 cups) water

3 green onions, coarsely chopped

2 carrots, peeled, coarsely chopped

2 parsnips, peeled, coarsely chopped

2 celery stalks, coarsely chopped

1 cup parsley sprigs, coarsely chopped

1 1/2 teaspoons salt

1/2 teaspoon ground black pepper

HERBED MATZO BALLS

1/3 cup chicken fat (reserved from soup)

1/3 cup cold broth (reserved from homemade chicken soup)

6 large eggs, beaten

2 tablespoons minced fresh chives

1 tablespoon minced fresh dill

2 tablespoons minced fresh parsley

1 tablespoon fresh thyme leaves

1 tablespoon plus 1 1/2 teaspoons salt

1/8 teaspoon pepper

1 1/2 cups matzo meal

4 quarts water

MAKE 12 SERVINGS

To make the soup: Combine all ingredients in a large stockpot. Bring to a boil over medium-high heat. Reduce heat to medium-low and cover partially with lid. Cook until soup reduces by one third, about 4 hours. During cooking, skim chicken fat from top surface of soup. Reserve 1/3 cup chicken fat and 1/3 cup broth for matzo balls. Remove chicken parts from soup and discard. (Soup may be prepared 2 days in advance if covered and stored in the refrigerator. Reheat before serving.)

Meanwhile, to make the matzo balls: Melt chicken fat in a small bowl in the microwave. Cool for 5 minutes. Beat melted chicken fat, reserved broth, and eggs until fluffy. Add chives, dill, parsley, thyme, 1 1/2 teaspoons salt, and pepper and beat until blended. Using a wooden spoon, stir in matzo meal until thoroughly combined. Cover with plastic wrap and refrigerate at least 30 minutes. (Matzo mixture may be prepared 1 day in advance if covered and stored in the refrigerator.)

Bring water and 1 tablespoon salt to a boil in a large stockpot over medium-high heat. With moistened hands, form cold matzo mixture into balls using 1 tablespoon mixture per ball. Carefully add balls to boiling water, cover, and cook until slightly firm and tender, about 40 minutes. Makes about 20 balls.

Using a slotted spoon transfer matzo balls to individual soup bowls. Ladle hot chicken soup with vegetables into bowls over matzo balls. Serve immediately.

Orange Brisket with Carrot-Onion Stuffing

Everyone's mom makes the best brisket! Well, we know we can't compete with your mother, but we hope to offer a new orange twist to this Passover classic. Choose a thin, flat cut of brisket at least 8 × 10 inches to make a nice, large stuffed roll.

CARROT-ONION STUFFING
2 tablespoons olive oil

2 cloves garlic, minced

2 cups diced onions

2 cups diced carrots

1 tablespoon fresh thyme leaves

2 matzo sheets, finely crumbled

4 tablespoons margarine, melted

1/4 cup canned beef broth

1/4 teaspoon salt

1/8 teaspoon black pepper

ORANGE BRISKET
1 (5-pound) flat-cut brisket

2 tablespoons olive oil

1 teaspoon salt

1/2 teaspoon black pepper

2 teaspoons fresh thyme leaves

6 onions, quartered

2 cups canned beef broth

1/2 cup fresh orange juice

3 large carrots, peeled, cut into 1-inch chunks

3 pounds red potatoes, cut into 1 1/2-inch chunks

4 cloves garlic, peeled

MAKES 10 SERVINGS

To make Carrot-Onion Stuffing: Heat oil in a large skillet over medium heat. Add garlic, onions, carrots, and thyme and cook until onions soften, about 8 minutes. Place matzo crumbs in a large bowl. Stir in vegetables, margarine, beef broth, salt, and pepper until thoroughly combined.

Preheat oven to 350F (175C). To make Orange Brisket: Lay brisket flat on a work surface and rub inside of brisket with 1 tablespoon of the olive oil, ½ teaspoon of the salt, and ¼ teaspoon of the pepper. Spread stuffing mixture evenly over inside of brisket, leaving 1-inch border on all sides. Roll up brisket encasing stuffing inside and tie closed by wrapping with kitchen string (see Note). Rub brisket with remaining 1 tablespoon oil, ½ teaspoon salt, ¼ teaspoon pepper, and 1 teaspoon thyme. Place half of the onions in bottom of a large roasting pan. Place brisket in a large pan, seam side down, on top of onions. Top brisket with remaining onions. Pour 1 cup of the beef broth, and ¼ cup of the orange juice into pan. Bake, uncovered, about 1 hour, or until meat and onions begin to brown, basting occasionally.

Add carrots, potatoes, garlic, and remaining 1 teaspoon thyme to pan around brisket. Pour remaining 1 cup beef broth and ¼ cup orange juice over brisket. Cover pan with foil and cook, basting occasionally, 2½ to 3 hours, or until brisket is almost done and is very tender when pierced with a fork. Remove from oven and let brisket stand 30 minutes before carving.

Slice brisket roll crosswise and reassemble slices for a nice presentation on a large serving platter. Spoon vegetables from pan around brisket or into serving bowl. Spoon off fat from pan juices and serve juice on side in a gravy boat.

Mandelbrot Pear and Cashew Crisp

Although the price of a box of mandelbrot can be steep, it's definitely worth the money. The crisp, with its cookie crust, sweet pears, and cashews, is an ideal ending to this celebratory meal.

MANDELBROT CRUST AND TOPPING
3 cups coarse mandelbrot crumbs

⅓ cup margarine, melted

3 tablespoons sugar

1 egg, lightly beaten

PEAR AND CASHEW FILLING
2 tablespoons margarine

¾ cup water

1 teaspoon fresh lemon juice

½ cup sugar

1 teaspoon ground cinnamon

1 tablespoon potato starch

3 pears, peeled, cut in thick slivers

½ cup unsalted cashews, coarsely chopped

MAKES 12 SERVINGS

To make crust and topping: Grease a 9-inch pie pan with margarine. Mix together crumbs, margarine, sugar, and egg in a large bowl until thoroughly combined. Reserve half of mixture for topping. Press the remaining mixture in bottom and up side of pie pan. Chill, uncovered, for 30 minutes.

Preheat oven to 350F (175C). To make filling: Melt margarine in a large saucepan over medium heat. Stir in water, lemon juice, sugar, and cinnamon until combined. Slowly sprinkle potato starch into mixture, stirring constantly until smooth. Add pears and cashews and cook, stirring occasionally, until pears are very tender, 15 to 20 minutes.

Remove from heat and pour pear mixture over chilled crust in pie pan. Pack remaining crumb mixture in dollops around rim of crust and over top of pears. Bake 25 to 30 minutes, or until filling is bubbly and topping is golden brown.

Cool for 5 minutes and cut into wedges. Serve hot. Store leftovers covered in plastic wrap in the refrigerator. Bring to room temperature or heat before serving.

Heirloom Family Matzo Cover and Afikomen Wrap

FROM FABRIC STORE: ½ yard white cotton fabric, with a smooth surface; 1 yard colorful, washable fabric; needle; thread; fabric glue; gold decorative trim

FROM CRAFT OR OFFICE SUPPLY STORE: small paintbrush, iron-on photo transfer paper

Find an old family photo, which will be transferred onto the front of the matzo cover and a more recent photo of the children for the Afikomen wrap. Machine wash and iron the white and colored fabric. Cut 2 12-inch squares from white fabric and 6 12-inch squares from colored fabric. Along one edge of the colored fabric squares, fold fabric under ½ inch and fold again to make a hem. Be sure to fold into wrong side of fabric. Press fold with iron and sew along middle of fold with sewing machine. Repeat process with additional 5 colored fabric squares.

Lay a colored square right side up and place another colored fabric square right side down directly on top of square with hemmed edges aligned. Sew squares together, ½ inch from edge, along perimeter of three edges, but do not sew the hemmed edge. Turn fabric inside out to reveal a cloth pocket. Repeat process with four other colored fabric squares, making three pockets total. Set one pocket aside for the Afikomen wrap. Lay other two pockets directly on top of each other and sew pockets together by hand along three outer edges, but do not sew hemmed edges.

For our matzo cover pictured in this book, we went to a copy center and had our photo color-copied onto transfer paper and then they used a heat press to transfer the paper's image onto our white fabric. Call your local copy center before you purchase the iron-on transfer paper and find out if they can provide this service. Or purchase iron-on transfer paper and follow the manufacturer's instructions to transfer your photo onto iron-on transfer paper. You will have to color copy the image on the paper or scan the image from a computer and print it on the paper. Follow manufacturer's instructions and use your iron set at the suggested heat level to transfer the photo image onto the white fabric. Trim the fabric to a ¼-inch border around the image. Brush a light coat of fabric glue on back of the fabric image. Center the fabric on the front of the matzo cover and adhere to cover. Finish photo border by adhering gold trim around photo with fabric glue. You can also decorate the hemmed edge with gold trim. Repeat photo transfer process on the remaining cloth envelope for the Afikomen wrap.

Opposite page:
The table displays a matzo cover,
Afikomen wrap, and Haggadah covers.

Haggadah Book Covers

FROM STATIONERY OR CRAFT STORE: 1 (2-foot-square) sheet of sturdy, handmade paper; 1 (5 × 7-inch) decorative paper sheet

FROM HARDWARE STORE: at least 1-foot length, 22-gauge, copper wire; super glue

This craft is just like covering a schoolbook. Lay handmade paper right side down on a flat surface. Open the Haggadah and place on paper. Measure ¼ inch from top and bottom of book and mark lines. If paper has a rough texture, carefully tear along marked lines. Or cut just beyond lines, and fold along lines into back side of paper. Fold excess paper on sides of book around edge of front and back cover. Close book to adjust paper's fit. Form copper wire into a small Hebrew letter or Passover symbol. Use super glue to adhere copper form to small handmade paper sheet. Trim or tear sheet as if to frame symbol and super glue paper onto front cover of book.

A Colorful Family Easter

April 6, 1969

The Story of Easter

The celebration of Easter is rich in folklore from many cultures. At the onset of springtime, ancient Anglo-Saxons, for example, would hold a pagan festival honoring the goddess Eastra or Ostra. Idolized on earth as a rabbit, she was the deity of spring and renewal. Thus we see how the symbolism of Easter—such as the egg and the bunny—is associated with themes of rebirth and fertility. Pagans, people who worshiped many gods and sought pleasure in what most see as a hedonistic manner, cast the seeds for many of our holidays today. Easter, the Christian observance of the Resurrection of Jesus Christ, is believed be one of them.

By A.D. 200, Christian beliefs were gradually being accepted by many in society. When the age-old spring festival came around, Christians chose this time to remember the crucifixion and miraculous rebirth of their savior. Christianity tells us that Jesus Christ was ordered to be put to death by Pontius Pilate, a Roman governor, in A.D. 30. As we all know, He was nailed to a cross, suffered horribly, and three days later rose from the dead.

Coincidentally, the Resurrection took place during Passover, a Jewish

According to the United States Department of Agriculture, six hundred million eggs are sold in America during the Easter season (March and April) 2000.

APRIL
National Humor Month

National Karaoke Week (fourth week in April)

National Fun at Work Day (April 5)

celebration commemorating the "exodus of the Hebrews" enslaved in Egypt. Christians of the day had roots in Judaism and for a while Easter and Passover were celebrated together. During the fourth century, Christians began to observe Good Friday, the day of Christ's crucifixion. In A.D. 325, the Council of Nicaea ordained that Easter was to be celebrated on the Sunday on or after the first full moon of the spring equinox. Around this time Good Friday and Easter became Christian holidays and Passover solely Jewish.

Easter is the final event in a period of religious observances. Lent, a time of penitence and some fasting, begins forty days prior to Easter, and starts on Ash Wednesday. The day before is celebrated around the world as Mardi Gras and Carnival. Mardi Gras, French for "Fat Tuesday," is a raucous day of feasting before the solemnity of Lent. At the end of Lent, Holy Week begins with Palm Sunday, representing Jesus' return to Jerusalem. Then, Maundy Thursday symbolizes the Last Supper of Christ, followed by Good Friday and Easter Sunday.

Probably the most sacred holiday for Christians around the world, Easter is a divine celebration of life eternal.

Festive Traditions and Folklore

A few months after children hunted for Easter eggs, men were collecting rocks on the moon on July 20, 1969. While we can't deny that the groovy colors of this decade made Easter depicted in the '60s very attractive, there was a spiritual sense of strength and unity that Americans felt with that lunar touchdown.

Many paint this holiday with all the colors of the rainbow from the eggs to the decor. Friends and families often gather for a late-morning celebration during which adults feast and children look for Easter eggs. Some parents plan a scavenger hunt the night before with intricate clues leading to a big basket full of chocolate bunnies, marshmallow chicks, and jelly beans. We have some egg-cellent customs to share with you to help make your holiday out of this world!

Easter Eggs

Everything about the Easter egg sings spring! An obvious symbol of life, the brightly colored shells of these gems are reminiscent of flowers blooming in the new season. Believed to be a custom in ancient Egypt, Persia, Greece, and China, to name a few, people gave eggs as gifts at spring festivals. According to one old myth, the sun was a bird that was hatched from an "egg world"; and in another version the world emerged from a "universe egg."

Often the color of eggs and the way they are used have certain significance. Some orthodox Christians still practice a tradition of baking red-colored eggs into bread; red is symbolic of Christ's blood, and bread the staff of life. They bring the egg-encrusted bread to a midnight mass to be blessed, and on Easter morning give it to a friend or family member, usually a godparent.

For a time, eating eggs was forbidden during Lent. People would hard-boil eggs to save them until they could be eaten and given as gifts on Easter. Now a fun custom for children, dyeing eggs probably started as a way for families to teach children about the spiritual meaning of Easter. And as for the Easter egg hunt, what child's interest wouldn't be piqued by the promise of an adventure?

German villagers paint Easter eggs with patterns that have been in their families for generations. Austrians also make elaborate eggs by attaching a leaf to the egg before it is dyed. When the egg dries, the leaf is removed to reveal its image on the white shell. The Polish are renowned for making Pisnaki eggs, using a process of drawing a design on the egg in beeswax and several dips in dye. They make a gorgeous Easter treasure.

The Easter Bunny and His Candy

The rabbit, known for its fertility, is symbolic of the birth of spring. But the giant bunny who hops into our homes to fill baskets with candy and runs around the backyard planting eggs is another story! The Easter bunny is believed to have originated in sixteenth-century German literature. When Germans emigrated to America two hundred years later, they brought the tradition of the *Osterhase* (Easter bunny) with them. Children

In 1885, Czar Alexander III commissions master jeweler Peter Carl Fabergé to make a fabulously bejeweled imperial Easter egg as an Easter day surprise for his wife, Czarina Maria Gydorovna. She loves the gift so much that the czar commissioned fifty-six more. The current value for a single imperial egg is about $6 million.

The jelly bean pops onto the scene in 1861. An advertisement promotes the sending of jelly bean treats to soldiers in the Union Army. By 1998, jelly bean consumption for the Easter season totals fifteen billion. If these beans are lined up end to end they will circle the globe almost three times.

would make nests in their hats and bonnets and the folkloric rabbit would place colored eggs in them. As the ritual developed, decorated baskets replaced the homemade nests. Germans have been making bunny-shaped confections and pastry since the nineteenth century. Happily, chocolate candy eggs and bunnies found their way into the baskets, making the custom of the Easter bunny extra sweet for kids.

Easter Parades

In 1933, Irving Berlin's song "Easter Parade" romanticized this age-old holiday tradition. What seems like a modern excuse for a shopping spree is somewhat of a social rite of spring. Dating back to the Middle Ages, people of many cultures would strut their new fineries on their way to church or visiting friends on Easter Sunday. A more spiritual meaning of this ritual holds that it represents the procession that followed Christ carrying the cross. The Atlantic City Easter parade, started in 1860, was a grand promenade. People would dress in elegant hats and brand-new clothes to take their customary stroll down the boardwalk. Fifth Avenue in New York City enjoys its fair share of fashionable traffic on the holiday, as does Dupont Circle in Washington, D.C., which started its parade in 1952.

White House Easter Egg Roll

Perhaps the most time-honored tradition for children in Washington, D.C. is the White House Easter Egg Roll. Dolly Madison is usually credited for initiating this Easter Monday event sometime between 1809 and 1817. Originally families with young children would roll Easter eggs, colored by the children of the president and staff, across the lawn of the Capitol. As this activity took its toll on the grounds, the tradition stopped in 1876. There is a tale of how children armed with Easter baskets confronted President Rutherford B. Hayes in protest of the cancellation of the event. The president and his wife were charmed by the kids and reinstated the tradition in 1878. Since then, children accompanied by an adult roll eggs on the lush South Lawn of the White House, unless poor weather conditions or war cause the event to be canceled. As a souvenir, each child receives a wooden egg signed by the current president and first lady.

Easter Brunch for Twelve

The sixties are remembered as a wild time of artistic expression, political activism, and fantastic food. Famed chef Julia Child brought culinary wonders into our homes with her TV show, and with the Immigration Act of 1968, the country experienced an influx of new and tasty ethnic food. With such a vibrant decade as our template, we've designed an Easter celebration full of creative and traditional holiday food.

Many dine on ham or turkey at their Easter table for either brunch or dinner. Our menu includes the favorites as well as some flavorful touches such as a sweet glaze on carved ham. We also have an Easter bread recipe with colored eggs baked in the top of the bread, as this tradition spans many cultures. While we respect the purity of plain Easter bread, we rejoice in the sweet life symbolized by a bread full of chocolate chips and cherries!

Brown Sugar, Ginger, and Maple-Glazed Ham

Roasted Red Pepper, Spinach, and Feta Egg Tart

Fresh Fruit with Light Apricot Sauce

Chocolate Chip and Cherry Easter Bread

Coffee and Fruit Juices

Brown Sugar, Ginger, and Maple-Glazed Ham

Purchase ham labeled "fully cooked" and preferably smoke-cured for this recipe.

1 (8-pound) fully cooked, bone-in, smoke-cured half ham (shank end)

1 tablespoon peeled, minced fresh ginger

1/2 cup maple syrup

2 tablespoons cider vinegar

1/4 cup firmly packed light brown sugar

MAKES 12 SERVINGS

Preheat oven to 350F (175C). Trim the fat on outside of ham to a 1/4-inch-thick layer. Score surface into diamonds. Insert a meat thermometer into thickest part of ham. Place ham on a wire rack in a roasting pan and bake 45 minutes.

Combine ginger, maple syrup, and vinegar in a small bowl. Brush glaze over surface of ham. Pack brown sugar over glaze. Bake 30 minutes and baste ham with glaze. Bake 15 to 30 minutes more, or until meat thermometer registers 140F (60C).

Transfer ham to a wooden cutting board and let stand 15 minutes. Place carving board on buffet table and carve into thin slices as needed.

Roasted Red Pepper, Spinach, and Feta Egg Tart

For those who want the breakfast side of brunch, this scrumptious and colorful egg tart looks as good as it tastes. Frozen spinach is a convenient ingredient used in this recipe, but be sure to squeeze out all excess water or your tart may have a green tint. Although this recipe yields 12 servings, you may wish to make an extra tart for those among your guests who want seconds.

TART CRUST

1½ cups all-purpose flour

¼ teaspoon salt

½ cup unsalted butter, chilled, cut into ½-inch cubes

1 egg

2 to 3 tablespoons ice water

TART FILLING

1 tablespoon olive oil

1 red bell pepper

¾ cup chopped cooked fresh or thawed frozen spinach; squeeze out all excess water

⅓ cup freshly grated Parmesan cheese

¾ cup crumbled feta cheese

3 eggs

¾ cup half-and-half

¼ teaspoon salt

⅛ teaspoon white pepper

MAKES 12 SERVINGS

To make the crust: Combine flour, salt, butter, and egg in a food processor. Pulse until just combined and butter forms pea-sized pieces. With processor running, slowly add cold water through feed tube until dough just holds together. Form dough into a thick disk, cover in plastic, and chill 1 hour.

Preheat oven to 425F (220C). Roll out chilled pastry to a ¼-inch thickness on a heavily floured surface. Line a 12-inch tart pan with removable bottom with pastry and trim edges. Pierce crust bottom several times with fork. Place pie weights or dry beans over surface of crust to weigh down during cooking process. Bake crust 10 minutes, or until lightly browned. Remove from oven.

To make the tart: Preheat oven to 450F (235C). Spread oil in a baking pan. Cut off stem and remove seeds from pepper. Slice pepper in half lengthwise and place, cut side down, in prepared baking pan. Roast for 10 minutes and turn pepper over. Roast 10 to 15 minutes more, or until extremely tender and skin is slightly wrinkled or blackened. Cool completely. Peel off outer skin and slice pepper into slivers.

Reduce oven temperature to 375F (190C). Set tart pan on a jelly-roll pan in case filled tart leaks during baking. Scatter half of the feta and Parmesan cheeses over bottom of crust. Scatter pepper slivers and spinach in an even layer over cheese. Whisk together eggs, half-and-half, salt, and white pepper until blended. Pour mixture over pepper and spinach. Top with remaining cheese. Bake 35 to 40 minutes, or until puffed. Remove from oven and cool for 5 minutes to allow tart to set.

NOTE Here's an easy way to line a tart pan or pie plate to avoid pastry tearing. Roll out pastry to desired thickness. Then, starting at end of pastry nearest you, roll up pastry around rolling pin. Hold rolling pin over edge of pie plate and unroll pastry over pie plate.

Remove rim of pan. Cut the tart into wedges and serve warm. Store any leftovers, covered in plastic wrap, in the refrigerator up to 2 days.

Fresh Fruit with Light Apricot Sauce

Elegant and light, this sauce is lovely on fruit at a summertime brunch.

1/4 cup apricot preserves or jam

1/2 cup fresh orange juice

3/4 cup water

1/4 cup minced dried apricots

2 oranges, peeled, cut in sections

2 bananas, sliced crosswise

2 cups 1-inch cubes honeydew melon

1 cup diced fresh pineapple

1 cup chopped apples

1 cup fresh seasonal berries

MAKES 12 SERVINGS

Cook apricot preserves, orange juice, water, and apricots in a medium saucepan over medium-high heat, stirring occasionally, until preserves are melted and mixture is combined, about 5 minutes. Cool to room temperature.

Place fruit in a large bowl and pour apricot sauce over fruit. Toss lightly to coat and serve lightly chilled.

Chocolate Chip and Cherry Easter Bread

Use nontoxic dye when coloring the eggs, as the dye may rub off on the bread (see Note). Also, the eggs are raw when dyed, as opposed to the traditional method for coloring Easter eggs in which they are initially hard-cooked. Finally, we suggest storing this bread in the refrigerator to keep the encrusted eggs safe for consumption. If the bread happens to stay out overnight or on a shaded brunch table for more than 2 hours, remove the eggs and discard to prevent anyone from eating them.

1/4 cup sugar

1 (1/4-ounce) package active dry yeast (about 1 tablespoon)

1 teaspoon salt

3 cups all-purpose flour

2/3 cup warm milk

2 tablespoon unsalted butter, softened

2 eggs

1/3 cup dried cherries, chopped

1/3 cup semisweet chocolate chips

1/3 cup slivered almonds

1/2 teaspoon anise seeds

1 tablespoon canola oil

5 uncooked eggs, colored with nontoxic Easter egg dye

MAKES 1 LOAF

Combine sugar, yeast, salt, and 1 cup of the flour in a large bowl. Heat milk and butter in a small saucepan over low heat until milk is lukewarm 110F (45C) and butter has melted. Pour milk into dry ingredients and beat well about 2 minutes. Add eggs and ½ cup of the flour and beat another 2 minutes, or until batter thickens.

Add remaining 1½ cups flour and stir until dough pulls away from side of bowl. Turn out dough onto a lightly floured surface and knead until dough is smooth and elastic but not sticky, 10 minutes. Use more flour if necessary.

Oil a large clean bowl and transfer dough into it. Turn dough over once to oil top of dough. Cover bowl tightly with plastic wrap and place in a warm, draft-free area. Let dough stand until it doubles in size, about 2 hours.

Butter a baking sheet. Combine the dried cherries, chocolate chips, and anise seeds in a small bowl. Punch down the dough in bowl and turn out onto a lightly floured surface. Knead in the cherry and chocolate chip mixture until incorporated throughout dough.

Divide the dough in half. Roll each half into a 2-foot-long rope. Loosely twist the 2 ropes together and form into a ring on a prepared baking sheet. Pinch ends together to close ring. Carefully push apart twists in ropes to make a place for each egg. Gently push eggs down into openings in ropes as deep as possible. Loosely cover bread with waxed paper and let rise in a warm, draft-free area until bread doubles in size, about 1 hour.

HOMEMADE EASTER EGG DYE Combine 1 cup water with 1 teaspoon white wine vinegar. Stir in food coloring by drops until liquid is desired color. Immerse eggs in dye 30 minutes, turning occasionally. Pat eggs dry with paper towels before adding to dough.

Preheat oven to 350F (175C). Brush surface of bread and Easter eggs with canola oil. Bake 25 to 30 minutes, or until a toothpick inserted in bread comes out clean. Place on a wire rack to cool.

Easter Egg Stencils on
Sod Squares As Lawn Decor

FROM NURSERY: 3 (4 × 2-foot) sod strips with mesh backing and grass blades that are 1 inch high

FROM CRAFT STORE: 4 cans pastel-colored spray paint; 6 (4-fluid ounce) bottles different colors acrylic paint; 1-inch-wide paintbrush; ½-inch-wide paintbrush

Cut sod pieces into 2-foot squares. Make sure grass is not wet prior to painting. Make an oval egg stencil, 1½ feet long and proportionately wide, from cardboard. Place stencil on sod square and spray-paint a pastel-colored egg on square. Repeat process with additional squares, painting each a different color. Allow paint to dry. Spray an additional coat on each egg; let dry completely. Using acrylic paint and paintbrush, create Easter egg designs or bright-colored stripes, polka dots, and zigzags on painted eggs. Allow paint to dry and set squares on lawn as decor. (NOT RECOMMENDED FOR A RAINY DAY.)

Flower Easter Bunny and
Baby Chick in Colorful Grass Centerpiece

FROM CRAFT STORE: 2 (6.7-liter) bags green sphagnum moss; Tack 2000 wet floral spray adhesive; 1 large cake pan shaped like an Easter bunny; 1 large cake pan shaped like an Easter chick; 5 or 6 bricks green floral Oasis; 2 each of the following-diameter plant saucers: 4 inches, 6 inches, and 8 inches; 1 yard sheer pink ribbon; 1 (7-inch-long, 22-gauge) green floral wire; plastic wrap

FROM FLORIST: 50 white carnations; 10 pink carnations; 70 yellow spider chrysanthemums; 2 orange calendula blooms; 2 purple statice sprays; 3 yellow Solidaster sprays; 30 stems assorted spring flowers; 40 Galax leaves

FROM HEALTH-FOOD STORE: 2 (16-inch-square) flats of wheat grass with long blades

The day before you make this craft, soak moss in water to rid it of dust and revive green color. Wring moss

Opposite page:
An Easter bunny and baby chick
are created using flowers.

thoroughly dry with hands. Spray backs of bunny and chick pans with Tack 2000 floral adhesive. Cover backs of pans by adhering thin layer of moss with Tack 2000.

Pack Oasis into bunny and chick cake pans, trimming bricks as necessary to fit. Pack 6 plant saucers with Oasis. Trim Oasis in containers so it is level with rims of pans and saucers. Pour water into pans and saucers to soak Oasis. Spray Tack 2000 over Oasis in saucers only and adhere thin layer of moss to Oasis until it is covered.

To make bunny, cut white and pink carnation stems to 1½-inch lengths. Insert white carnation stems side by side in bunny pan Oasis so carnations form shape of bunny. Use pink carnations to make bunny tail, nose, and inside of ear. Cut stems below 3 purple statice blooms to 1½-inch lengths and insert in bunny for eye. Tie a bow using pink ribbon. Using wire cutters, cut green floral wire to 3-inch lengths. Bend wire around pink bow in hairpin shape and insert wire ends into bunny's neck area. Insert Galax leaf stems into Oasis around perimeter to outline bunny.

To make chick, cut yellow chrysanthemum stems, calendula stems, and 5 stems below purple statice blooms to 1½-inch lengths. Insert chrysanthemum stems side by side into chick pan Oasis to form shape of chick. Insert orange calendula stems for eyes and purple statice for beak. Cut stems on yellow Solidaster blooms to 3-inch lengths and insert for chick wing. Insert Galax leaf stems into Oasis around perimeter to outline chick.

Cut assorted spring flower stems to varying lengths and insert in plant saucers so arrangements resemble a garden.

Lay sheets of plastic wrap over center of table, covering a 4-foot-square area. Place 1 square of wheat grass in center of table over plastic. Place flower bunny and chick pans flat on table or prop slightly upright by leaning against a garden rock. (Do not stand pans on end, because arrangement may come away from pan.) Arrange plant saucers with spring flowers around bunny and chick. Fill spaces in between pans and saucers with clumps of wheat grass, rearranging saucers as necessary. Place wheat grass around the perimeter of centerpiece, giving it a curvy outer edge as opposed to an even circle. Trim or tuck under plastic and neaten for finished look.

Opposite page:
Feathered Easter baskets and lilies
are arranged on stenciled grass.

The Feathered Nest Easter Basket

For each basket, buy the following:

FROM CRAFT STORE: 1 basket with a handle; 2 (½-ounce) bags colored feathers; hot glue; 1 (2-foot) strand of plastic stringed beads

Using hot glue, adhere feathers around the outside and inside of the basket and up around the handle. Glue a strand of plastic beads over the feathers wrapped around the basket's handle.

CAUTION: Do not use hot glue if you intend to make this craft with kids. Substitute white glue, which may not have the longevity of hot glue but will be much safer.

Ladies on
Mother's Day

May 10, 1914

The Story of Mother's Day

Although Mother's Day became a national holiday in 1914, the custom of honoring mother has stretched over centuries. In ancient Greece, a spring festival for Rhea, the mother of many deities, was celebrated. The Romans regaled their god Cybele in the same fashion. Christians feted the Virgin Mary, mother of Christ, on the fourth Sunday in Lent by decorating churches with flowers and treasures.

England was one of the first countries to establish a day for mum as "Mothering Sunday." This holiday, which started as a religious remembrance of the Virgin Mother, then grew to include all mothers. Children went "a-mothering," heading to the nearest big city and coming home with flowers and sweet gifts for mom.

One of the first American accounts of a day for mothers was in 1872 at the behest of Julie Ward Howe, lyricist of "The Battle Hymn of the Republic." Mother's Day observances were celebrated regionally throughout the late nineteenth century, but it was a schoolteacher named Anna Jarvis who brought the holiday to the national forefront. Anna's mother

MAY

National Barbecue Month

International Pickle Week (week before and including Memorial Day Weekend)

National Tap Dance Day (May 25)

was an admirable woman who, during the Civil War, organized groups called Mother's Day Work Clubs that were devoted to making conditions for fighting soldiers more comfortable and hygienic. Mrs. Jarvis, showing no favoritism to either the North or South, arranged a Mothers' Friendship Day in 1865 at which parties from both sides attended and acted with civility. The success of the original celebration led to the day becoming an annual event.

On May 9, 1905, Anna Jarvis's mother died. This strengthened Anna's determination to have a national day set aside for mothers. In 1908, after countless letters to the government requesting this special day, the church where Anna's mother taught Sunday school honored her mother by tolling a bell seventy-two times, one for each year of her life. White carnations, being the favorite flower of the late Mrs. Jarvis, were handed out in her memory.

By 1911, most states were celebrating their own version of Mother's Day. In December 1912, the Mother's Day International Association was formed, which furthered the promotion of the day. Finally, in 1914, President Woodrow Wilson proclaimed the second Sunday in May as Mother's Day. We set aside this day to pamper, adore, and celebrate the woman who gave us life.

Festive Traditions and Folklore

We've chosen the year 1914 for our Mother's Day celebration, as this was when the observance first became a national holiday. The long-standing British tradition of an afternoon tea seems more than appropriate for this day, since the English were one of the first to celebrate "Mothering Sunday."

Just as each of our moms has her own special way about her, so the customs surrounding the day are unique to each family. Some celebrations are silly, with Mom wearing a paper crown made by the kids and is dubbed "Queen for a Day." Some are indulgent, and mom is sent on an all-day spa excursion. And some are sweet, as mom awakes to a family chorus of "M is for the memories that you gave me . . ."

Breakfast in Bed

The classic Mother's Day morning scene is of a kitchen that looks like a tornado hit it with dad and the kiddies balancing a breakfast tray en route to mom's bedroom. A delicate bud vase with a single flower is the finishing touch for this gift from the heart and from little, floured hands.

Corsage for Mom

Mom at the home prom! The custom of corsages for moms hasn't been as popular over the years, but we think it should be revived. Not only does a flower corsage make mom feel special, but it brings back nostalgic occasions like a high-school prom or a wedding that will make her feel all warm and fuzzy.

Mrs. Robinson (Anne Bancroft): In the late sixties, the woman every guy hoped his mom would befriend.

Mr. Mom (Michael Keaton): He made overtaxed moms everywhere sit back, relax, and laugh knowingly during the early 1980s.

Elizabeth Ann Buttle: She gave birth to a daughter, Belinda, in 1956 and a son, Joseph, in 1997, thus becoming the Guinness World Record title holder for the longest interval (forty-one years) between births. She was sixty when her son was born, also making her the oldest "new" mother in Britain.

Mother's Day Tea for Four

There is an intimacy between a mother and child that we thought would be beautifully illustrated with a quaint afternoon tea. Most families go out to brunch or serve mom breakfast in bed for this holiday and are ready for a little snack in the late afternoon.

Teatime has been a cherished ritual for the English for hundreds of years no matter where they eventually call home. Many believe that "high tea" is reserved for "high-class" people. Actually, the terms "high" and "low," when speaking of teatime, refer more to the hour when the tea is served. Traditionally, it is the upper classes that serve a "low" or "afternoon" tea around 4 P.M. The menu is similar to the one we offer here of finger food, scones, and sweets. Middle and lower classes have a "high" tea later in the day, around dinnertime, and the heartier food is reserved for the evening meal.

Herb and Cheese
Diamonds

Cucumber-Wrapped
Smoked Salmon and
Cream-Cheese Rolls

Almond Scones with
Gourmet Jams

Flowerpot Peaches and
Cream Shortcake

A Pot of Tea

Herb and Cheese Diamonds

A delicate morsel of fresh herbs and cheese on diamond-shaped bread slices is just right with a spot of tea.

1/4 cup minced watercress leaves

4 tablespoons minced fresh parsley

1/4 cup minced fresh basil leaves

16 thin slices white bread

3 tablespoons butter, melted

1/4 teaspoon salt

1/8 teaspoon white pepper

1/2 cup (3 ounces) port wine cheese spread, softened

1/2 cup (4 ounces) mascarpone cheese, softened (see Note below)

5 cherry tomatoes, thinly sliced

MAKES 4 SERVINGS

Preheat oven to 350F (175C). Toss together watercress and 2 tablespoons of the parsley in a small bowl until combined. In another small bowl, toss together basil and remaining 2 tablespoons parsley until combined. Set aside.

Cut 3 × 2-inch diamond shapes from bread slices using a diamond-shaped cookie cutter or a sharp knife. Brush both sides of diamonds with melted butter. Place on a baking sheet and sprinkle with salt and pepper. Toast for 4 minutes, or until light brown.

Spread 1 tablespoon port wine cheese spread over each of 8 diamonds. Spread 1 tablespoon mascarpone cheese over each of the remaining 8 diamonds. Sprinkle watercress mixture over port-wine-cheese-spread-topped diamonds and basil mixture over mascarpone cheese-topped diamonds. Or make a design with herbs such as stripes across diamond. Garnish with a cherry tomato slice in center of each diamond.

Return to oven and cook 5 to 8 minutes, or until cheese is melted. Arrange on serving tray and serve immediately.

NOTE Mascarpone cheese is usually available at Italian delicatessens or gourmet markets. If unavailable, mix together 1/3 cup cream cheese with 1 tablespoon sour cream and 1 tablespoon heavy cream until blended. Makes 1/2 cup mock mascarpone cheese.

Cucumber-Wrapped Smoked Salmon and Cream-Cheese Rolls

In lieu of the customary cucumber tea sandwiches, this recipe presents a sheer slice of cucumber encasing salmon and seasoned cream cheese.

1 (8-ounce) package cream cheese, softened

2 teaspoons fresh lemon juice

1 tablespoon capers

1 tablespoon minced fresh dill

6 ounces cold-smoked salmon or lox, thinly sliced

1 English cucumber, peeled, thinly sliced lengthwise

16 dill sprigs, for garnish

MAKES 4 SERVINGS

Whip cream cheese in a medium bowl until smooth. Stir in lemon juice, capers, and dill until combined.

Cut salmon into 4 × 1-inch strips. Trim cucumber slices to same size as salmon strips. Lay 1 salmon strip on top of each cucumber strip. Place ½ teaspoon cheese mixture on one end of each salmon strip. Starting from cream-cheese end, roll up strips, enclosing cheese inside. Secure rolls by spreading a dab of cheese on loose end of strip and in between salmon and cucumber strips. Press to adhere end to roll (or insert wooden pick through roll to secure end).

Set rolls, cream-cheese side up, on a serving tray. Place a small dill sprig on cream cheese and serve. (May be made 1 day in advance if covered in plastic wrap and stored in the refrigerator.)

Almond Scones with Gourmet Jams

Scones are a classic on any teatime menu, but we've spiced these up by adding dried fruit and goodies to store-bought jams. A gift of these jams would be lovely for any mom.

2 cups all-purpose flour

1/4 cup sugar

1 tablespoon baking powder

1/8 teaspoon salt

1/2 cup unsalted butter, chilled, coarsely chopped

3 tablespoons almond paste, broken into small pieces

3/4 cup chopped unsalted almonds

1 egg

1 egg yolk

2/3 cup plus 2 tablespoons heavy cream

GOURMET JAMS
1/2 cup apricot jam

3 tablespoons finely chopped dried cranberries

1/2 cup strawberry jam

3 tablespoons finely chopped dried peaches

1/2 cup blackberry jam

2 tablespoons minced crystallized ginger

MAKES ABOUT 12 SCONES

Preheat oven to 425F (220C). Line a baking sheet with waxed paper and lightly spray paper with nonstick cooking spray.

Combine flour, sugar, baking powder, salt, butter, almond paste, and almonds in a food processor and process until mixture resembles coarse crumbs. Pour mixture into a large bowl.

Whisk together egg, egg yolk, and 2/3 cup cream until blended. Stir egg mixture into flour mixture until dough just begins to hold together. Turn out dough onto a lightly floured surface and with lightly floured hands pat dough to 1/2-inch thickness. Cut out scones using a 2-inch-diameter heart-shaped cookie cutter or round biscuit cutter. Gather excess dough and repeat process. Place scones 3 inches apart on prepared baking sheet.

Lightly brush surface of scones with remaining 2 tablespoons cream. Bake 15 to 20 minutes, or until puffed and golden brown. Remove from oven and cool on wire rack.

Meanwhile, to make jams: Mix together apricot jam and cranberries in a small bowl. Mix together strawberry jam and peaches in another small bowl. Mix together blackberry jam and ginger in another small bowl. Place each jam mixture in a small ceramic pot or decorative container.

Place scones in a cloth-napkin-lined basket and serve with jams.

Flowerpot Peaches and Cream Shortcake

We've substituted a genoise, similar to a sponge cake, as the cake layer for this classic dessert. The strawberry has also been nudged aside for fresh peaches. Buy 4 (1-cup-capacity) new glazed ceramic flowerpots with plastic liners for this recipe

GENOISE LAYERS

4 eggs, separated

1 cup sugar

2 tablespoons butter, melted

2 tablespoons fresh orange juice

1 cup cake flour

1 teaspoon baking powder

1/8 teaspoon salt

PEACHES AND CREAM FILLING

3 medium ripe peaches, washed, pitted, cut into thin wedges

3 tablespoons granulated sugar

1/2 teaspoon ground cinnamon

2 cups heavy cream

Nasturtium flowers (see Note below)

1/3 cup powdered sugar

MAKES 4 SERVINGS

To make the genoise: Center a rack in the oven and preheat oven to 350F (175C). Butter a 15 × 10-inch jelly-roll pan and line pan with waxed paper. Butter and flour waxed paper, shaking off excess flour.

Beat egg yolks and 1/2 cup of the sugar in a medium bowl until pale yellow. Add melted butter and orange juice and beat until blended. In another large bowl, using clean beaters, beat egg whites on high speed until soft peaks form. Gradually add remaining 1/2 cup sugar and beat until stiff peaks form. Fold yolk mixture into egg whites. Sift together dry ingredients and gently fold into mixture.

Pour mixture into prepared jelly-roll pan and smooth top surface with a rubber spatula. Bake for 12 minutes, or until center springs back to the touch. Remove from oven and cool in pan 5 minutes on a wire rack.

Lay a sheet of waxed paper on a cutting board. Trim 1/4 inch off all sides of cake, using a sharp knife. Lift waxed paper under cake away from pan and invert onto clean waxed paper on cutting board. Peel waxed paper away from cake.

Wash and dry flowerpots and liners. Place liners in pots. Cut 4 rounds from sponge cake to fit in bottom of flowerpots. Cut 4 rounds for a middle cake layer in pots. Cut 4 rounds to fit as a top cake cover just below the rim of pots. Cover and set aside.

To make the filling: Toss together peaches, 1 tablespoon granulated sugar, and cinnamon in a large bowl until combined. In another bowl, whip heavy cream and remaining 2 tablespoons granulated sugar until thick.

To assemble: Set bottom cake rounds in each flowerpot. Fill pots one-third of the way up with peaches and a dollop of whipped cream. Place middle cake rounds on cream in each pot. Fill pots two-thirds of the way up with peaches and a dollop of whipped cream. Place top cake rounds on cream and gently press until level with top rim of pots. Top with a dollop of whipped cream and garnish with a couple of nasturtium flowers. Place flowerpots on individual plates and sift powdered sugar over top. Serve immediately or refrigerate up to 1 hour.

NOTE Edible nasturtium flowers can be found in the produce section of gourmet grocery stores.

Mother's Day Decor and Personal Touches

Floating Flowers in a Tabletop Fountain

FROM CRAFT STORE: 1 small, battery-operated fountain pump with ¼-inch wide tubing adapter; ¼-inch-wide plastic tubing (2-foot length); 1 (1-foot-) diameter ceramic or glass bowl that is at least 2 inches deep; 1 block dry floral foam; 15 polished rocks; 3 (12-inch-long 22-gauge) green floral wires; mini-watering can or tiny bucket (some items may also be found at an aquarium store)

FROM FLORIST OR PLANT NURSERY: 1 baby ivy plant with 2-foot long vines; 15 stems assorted spring flowers (or select silk ivy and flowers for a permanent display)

FROM HARDWARE STORE: 1 (20-inch) piece green, solid, 12-gauge insulated wire

Assemble fountain pump according to manufacturer's instructions, using ¼-inch wide plastic tubing with adaptor. Place pump in ceramic bowl with battery pack on outside of bowl on table. Bend insulated wire into an arch. Cut floral foam into 2 (2-inch) cubes. Insert each end of wire arch into center of a cube and stand arch in bowl. Completely cover pump and weigh down foam cubes with rocks. Run plastic tube connected to pump along back of arch and up to the middle of curve. Make sure tube has enough slack so it does not disconnect from pump. Using wire cutters, cut 2 green floral wires to 2-inch lengths. Fasten tube to the top middle of the arch and along side of the arch, using twisted floral wire. Allow tube to extend down from arch by 3 inches and cut tube.

Cut 2-foot-long ivy vines from plant. Wrap ivy up and around arch for decoration and to mask tubing. Wrap ivy around 3-inch extension, securing it with floral wire. Use remaining green floral wire to hang a miniature watering can or tiny bucket from middle of arch. Wire should be behind ivy, and plastic tube should be rigged to trickle water into watering can. Fill bowl with enough water so pump is totally immersed. Cut 10 spring flower stems to 2-inch lengths and insert into ivy around arch to decorate. Float remaining 5 spring flowers in water. Turn fountain on and mask battery pack on table with cloth or napkin. (Make this fountain with silk ivy and flowers to keep it as permanent décor.)

Opposite page:
Flowers and a mini-watering can are
used to form a tabletop fountain.

Flower Napkin Fold

Use a cotton napkin as polyester blends will not hold the fold well. Place napkin right side down on a flat surface. Fold all four corners into center of napkin. Fold newly formed four corners into the center of napkin. Gently turn the napkin over and fold four corners again into center of napkin. Place fingers on four points in center, holding them in place. With other hand, reach under corner of napkin and pull up on pointed flap. Flap will fold up, forming a petal around corner. Repeat this process at the 3 remaining corners. Continue to hold down the center points and reach between the petals to pull up 4 more pointed flaps. Place a real flower in the napkin flower's center.

Flowery "Mom" Sugar Cubes

Divide white canned frosting into small bowls and color mixture in each bowl with different shades of food coloring. Spoon mixture into a pastry bag fitted with a writing tip and pipe a letter on one side of each sugar cube so the letters will spell "Mom" or a name when cubes are placed next to each other. Decorate additional sugar cubes by piping flowers and designs on cube sides.

Gentlemen on Father's Day

June 21, 1936

The Story of Father's Day

Probably the youngest holiday in this book is the one dedicated to dear old Dad. It was Sonora Louise Smart Dodd's devotion to her dad that began the notion of a Father's Day in 1909. Sonora's father was a man to be admired in that he raised a family of five after his wife died in childbirth. Papa Dodd's birthday was on June 5, so Sonora thought this to be the perfect time for a day in honor of fathers and approached church officials with the idea. Due to Sonora's efforts, Father's Day was observed in Spokane, Washington, on the third Sunday in June, not quite on Dodd's father's birthday but close enough. Dodd wished for all to wear a red rose to honor fathers who were living and a white rose for those whose fathers had passed away.

Within the next few years Father's Day celebrations took place around Washington State. Small regional observances occurred around the country as well with one dated as early as 1908 in West Virginia. In 1915, Harry Meek, of the Chicago Lion's Club began promoting the holiday, also suggesting that the third Sunday in June be set aside for fathers. Meek

JUNE

National Accordion Awareness Month

Take Your Pet to Work Week (third week of June)

National Yo-Yo Day (June 6)

Some famous dads, real and fictional, who celebrate this day are:

George Washington: Born in 1732, he was the first president of the United States of America and the father of our country.

Daddy Warbucks: Adoptive father of Little Orphan Annie, he is rich, powerful, bald, and fun; what more could anyone want from a father?

Father Edward Flanagan: The founder of Boys Town, a home for orphaned, wayward, and/or troubled boys in 1917, Flanagan was famously portrayed by Spencer Tracy in the 1938 feature *Boys Town,* for which he won an Oscar

Jim Anderson (Robert Young): On *Father Knows Best,* he was the father every baby boomer watching television between 1954 and 1962 wanted for his very own.

attempted to get President Wilson to declare the day a holiday, but the president proclaimed only a national observance in 1916. President Coolidge also decreed that the nation observe the day in 1924, but still the holiday had not been "officially" set on the calendar.

A National Father's Day Committee was organized in New York City in 1936. Over the next thirty years many tried but failed to get an official stamp for Father's Day! Finally, in 1966, President Lyndon Johnson, with a later permanent resolution from President Nixon, made Dad's day official, giving him the third Sunday in June.

Festive Traditions and Folklore

The time period that we've chosen for this celebration of a picnic by the lake is 1936, the year the National Father's Day Committee was formed in New York City. Anyone who has traveled to The Big Apple and walked through Central Park has surely been struck by the contrast between the lush pathways and the stark, stone skyline. And in the middle of the oasis you'll find a twenty-two-acre lake with rowboats and toy boats skimming across its surface.

Sure Pop wants to relax on his day, but just as many dads are up for a rousing time out-of-doors. While we respect our fathers, we like to poke fun at them by giving gifts of singing Animatronic fish to mount on the wall and humorous mugs with a cheeky phrase on the front. Some present their dad with neckties, cards, and even flowers. Most run into his strong, supportive arms and give a big bear hug to the guy that gave them life.

The Necktie Is Going Strong!

Believe it or not, millions still buy a necktie for Dad on Father's Day. One of the only creative ways most dads have of expressing themselves at work, ties have been a male fashion accessory since 210 B.C. Apparently China's first emperor, Shih Huang Ti, wore a neckerchief, which some allow to pass for the first tie, and in 113 A.D., Roman emperor Trajan also made this stylish statement. How do we know about Trajan and Ti's ties? In the stone statues carved to memorialize these guys, they're wearing them.

Father of the Year Awards

Many organizations honor dads for their outstanding fathering achievements. The National Father's Day Committee gave a Father of the Year award, a tradition that continued for many years. Women's magazines, TV shows, and now Web sites run contests in which essays are written on "Why My Dad Should Be Father of the Year."

Father's Day Picnic for Six

We have a nice relaxing picnic in mind for Dad with hearty food fit for a king! A picnic can also offer an economical solution to a celebration since the great outdoors needs few embellishments. Times were hard during the 1930s, and families had to be creative in the kitchen. One-dish wonders such as macaroni and cheese were popular on the family table, as these meatless meal alternatives helped Depression-era families balance their budgets. Taking our cue from the "sandwich loaf," an innovative thirties luncheon special in which a variety of breads and fillings were assembled and then "frosted" to resemble a cake, we give you the Stacked Stromboli Ring Encrusted in Potato Basil Bread. Nothing's too good for Dad.

Stacked Stromboli
Ring Encrusted in
Potato Basil Bread

Artichoke, Eggplant,
and Pine Nut Ratatouille

Italian Parsley and
Lemon Pasta Salad

Iced Tea

Timeless and Sweet
Dad Bars

Stacked Stromboli Ring
Encrusted in Potato Basil Bread

This edible tribute to Dad's appetite is a takeoff on the muffuletta sandwich, which originated in New Orleans around 1906. The muffuletta is a mile-high sandwich stacked in bread as wide as a Frisbee. Our masterpiece is also sky-high, with the meat encased in a tasty bread ring.

POTATO BASIL DOUGH
2 medium potatoes, peeled, cut into 1-inch cubes

1 cup warm water (110F; 45C)

1 teaspoon sugar

1 (1/4-ounce) package active dry yeast (about 1 tablespoon)

2 3/4 cups bread flour

1 teaspoon salt

2 tablespoons finely chopped fresh basil

STROMBOLI FILLING
3/4 cup ricotta cheese, drained

1/4 cup freshly grated Parmesan cheese

1 egg

1 tablespoon chopped fresh basil

1/2 teaspoon salt

1/4 teaspoon pepper

1/4 cup olive oil

2 tablespoons red wine vinegar

1/2 teaspoon dried oregano

2 large tomatoes, thinly sliced

8 whole basil leaves (several leaves on a stem is fine)

1/2 pound thinly sliced pepperoni

1/2 pound thinly sliced mozzarella cheese

1 pound thinly sliced cappicola

1/2 pound thinly sliced provolone cheese

1 pound thinly sliced salami

MAKES 6 TO 8 SERVINGS

To make the dough: Place potatoes in a medium pot and cover with water. Bring to a boil over medium-high heat and cook until potatoes are tender, about 10 minutes. Drain in a colander and cool completely. Mash potatoes until smooth and force through a strainer into a bowl.

Add 2 teaspoons of the warm water, sugar, and yeast to a large bowl. Let stand until frothy, about 10 minutes.

Sift together flour and salt into a large bowl. Add potato, remaining water, and yeast mixture and stir until combined and mixture forms a soft dough. Turn out dough onto lightly floured surface and knead until dough is smooth and elastic, but not sticky, 10 minutes. Use more flour if necessary.

NOTE Do not eat leftover
stromboli that has been sitting
outside in hot weather.
Oil a large clean bowl and transfer dough into bowl. Cover bowl with plastic wrap and place in a warm, draft-free area. Let dough stand until it doubles in size, about 1 hour.

Turn out dough onto floured surface and knead until deflated. Knead in chopped basil until distributed
throughout dough. Set aside one-fourth of dough. Form larger piece of dough into an 18-inch circle, using
a floured rolling pin and floured fingers to gently stretch the edges. Form the smaller pieces of dough into
a 10-inch circle.

Preheat oven to 450F (230C) degrees.

To make stromboli filling: Combine ricotta cheese, Parmesan cheese, egg, chopped basil, 1/4 teaspoon of
the salt and 1/8 teaspoon of the pepper and mix well. In another medium bowl, whisk together oil, vinegar, oregano, remaining 1/4 teaspoon salt, and 1/8 teaspoon pepper. Add tomatoes and lightly toss to coat.

Generously oil the inside of a 12-cup Bundt pan. Press whole basil leaves artfully along the bottom and
halfway up side of pan, adhering leaves to oiled pan. Gently lift 18-inch dough circle over Bundt pan centered over middle tube. To line pan with dough, allow dough to drape from middle tube of Bundt pan down
into pan and up sides. Take care not to disturb the basil leaves. Lightly pat dough into place. Dough edges
should come up to outer rim of pan.

Layer stromboli ingredients in pan by spreading 1/4 cup ricotta mixture on dough in bottom of pan and top
with a single layer of tomato slices. Add a thick layer of pepperoni and then mozzarella. Spread another
1/4 cup ricotta mixture over top and another layer of tomato slices. Add a thick layer of capicola and then
provolone. Spread another 1/4 cup ricotta mixture over top and another layer of tomato slices. Add a thick
layer of salami. Spread remaining ricotta mixture over salami. Center the 10-inch dough circle over pan.
Pinch edges of dough in pan and top dough circle to completely seal stromboli. (It is not necessary to cut
a hole in the center of dough over pan tube.) Gather and trim excess dough around outer rim.

Bake 20 minutes, or until crust is light brown. Cool completely in pan and invert onto serving platter. Wrap
in plastic wrap before transporting to picnic site. Cut into wedges and serve at room temperature or
slightly warm. (Store wrapped in plastic in the refrigerator up to 2 days.)

Artichoke, Eggplant, and Pine Nut Ratatouille

This tangy side dish is great for a picnic as it is easily stored and transported in a canning jar, from which one can serve it as well.

5 tablespoons olive oil

2 cloves garlic, minced

1 large brown onion, coarsely chopped

1 red bell pepper, seeded, coarsely chopped

1 large eggplant, peeled, cut into ½-inch cubes

3 medium zucchini, coarsely chopped

1 cup coarsely chopped, drained, canned water packed artichoke hearts

⅓ cup pine nuts

1½ cups chopped canned tomatoes

1 tablespoon capers

1 tablespoon balsamic vinegar

¼ teaspoon salt

⅛ teaspoon black pepper

MAKES 6 SERVINGS

Heat 2 tablespoons of the oil in a large skillet over medium-high heat. Add garlic, onion, and bell pepper and cook until onion is transparent, about 5 minutes. Reduce heat to medium-low and add remaining 3 tablespoons oil, eggplant, and zucchini. Cover skillet and cook, stirring occasionally, for about 30 minutes. Stir in artichokes, pine nuts, tomatoes, and capers. Cook, uncovered, until the mixture thickens, 10 to 15 minutes. Remove from heat and stir in balsamic vinegar, salt, and pepper.

Cool to room temperature. Spoon into bowl and serve. (Store covered in plastic wrap up to 1 week in the refrigerator.)

Italian Parsley and Lemon Pasta Salad

This lively pasta salad will add color and zest to your celebration.

8 cups water

1½ teaspoons salt

¼ cup plus 2 tablespoons olive oil

1 pound bow tie pasta

1 green bell pepper, seeded, cut in slivers

1 red bell pepper, seeded, cut in slivers

2 cups coarsely chopped broccoli florets

1 (15-ounce) can baby corn on the cob, coarsely chopped

3 tablespoons finely chopped Italian parsley leaves

2 tablespoons fresh lemon juice

1 tablespoon balsamic vinegar

¼ teaspoon black pepper

MAKES 4 TO 6 SERVINGS

Bring water, 1 teaspoon of the salt, and 1 tablespoon of the oil to boil in a large pot over medium-high heat. Add pasta and cook until pasta is just tender, 8 to 10 minutes. Drain in a colander and cool. Transfer to a large bowl.

Heat the remaining 1 tablespoon oil in a large skillet over medium-high heat. Add bell peppers and broccoli, and cook, stirring occasionally, until vegetables soften, about 10 minutes. Add vegetables and baby corn to pasta.

Whisk together parsley, lemon juice, the ¼ cup oil, vinegar, black pepper, and remaining ½ teaspoon salt. Pour over pasta mixture and toss until thoroughly combined.

Serve at room temperature. (Store covered in plastic wrap in the refrigerator for up to 4 days.)

Timeless and Sweet Dad Bars

We've dubbed these bars timeless as many of the ingredients in the recipe have been around for a hundred years. Eagle brand gave us sweetened condensed milk in 1856. In 1904, C. H. Sumner introduced peanut butter to a thrilled public at the World's Fair Exposition in St. Louis. Oreos hit the scene in 1913, and in 1939, Nestlé's semisweet chocolate morsels revolutionized the cookie.

17 Oreo cookies

¼ cup unsalted butter, melted

¾ cup peanut butter

½ cup sweetened condensed milk

1 egg, lightly beaten

½ cup semisweet chocolate chips

½ cup chopped almonds

MAKES ABOUT 25 COOKIES

Scrape cream filling out of Oreo cookies and discard. Place cookies in a food processor and pulverize until finely ground.

Preheat oven to 350F (175C). Lightly spray an 8-inch-square baking pan with nonstick cooking spray. Place cookie crumbs into a mixing bowl and stir in butter until crumbs are thoroughly moistened. Pat crumb mixture into an even layer over bottom of prepared baking pan. Refrigerate for 30 minutes.

Beat together peanut butter, sweetened condensed milk, and egg until blended. Spread peanut butter mixture over chilled cookie crust. Sprinkle chocolate chips and almonds evenly over top.

Bake for 20 to 30 minutes, or until peanut butter appears dry. Cool thoroughly and refrigerate before cutting into 1-inch squares. (Store in an airtight container in freezer or refrigerator for up to 1 week.)

Painted Canvas Picnic Blanket

FROM ART STORE: 2 yards (54-inch-wide) primed canvas

FROM CRAFT STORE: 2 (4-fluid-ounce) bottles red acrylic paint; 5 (4-fluid-ounce) bottles assorted colors acrylic paint; 1-inch-wide paintbrush and thin-tipped paintbrush; clear acrylic shellac spray

FROM HARDWARE STORE: 3 yards double-sided carpet tape

Work on a flat surface covered with plastic or a painter's drop cloth. Place canvas, primed-side-down, on covered surface. Lay a strip of carpet tape along each 54-inch-wide side. Fold in taped edge of canvas, adhering the tape to canvas on unprimed side for a finished edge. The 2-yard-long sides should already have a finished edge.

Turn canvas over so it is primed side up and flat. To make a checkered pattern, use a yardstick and mark every 13¼ inches along 54-inch-wide side. Draw straight lines in pencil at each marked point down length of canvas. Mark every 12-inch point along 2-yard-long side of canvas and draw straight lines across width of canvas.

Paint every other check with red acrylic paint. (Optional: Tape off checks for more even lines.) Under adult supervision have the father's children paint scenes in the checks that are not red. Allow paint to dry completely and spray a coating of clear acrylic shellac over painting in a well-ventilated area; dry completely before use. Transport canvas to picnic site rolled on cardboard tube to avoid wrinkles. This is decorative and for all to sit on, but use plates and containers under food. Do not eat food straight off painted canvas.

Opposite page:
The Dad and Me Memory book rests on a picnic blanket made by
using acrylic paint on canvas.

Dad and Me Memory Book

FROM OFFICE SUPPLY STORE: 1 pack of decorative paper with cardboard backing; glue stick or spray adhesive

FROM FABRIC STORE: 4 (1-inch-diameter) buttons; white elastic string; needle; cloth ribbon or shoelace; scrap decorative fabric

Cut decorative paper in half crosswise using a professional paper-cutting machine, usually available at a copy center. Cut a few sheets at a time and the cardboard by itself for an even cut. Assemble book with cardboard as front and back covers and pages in between. Book should lie with long side left to right. Measure 1½ inches from top and bottom of cardboard and ½ inch in from left margin. Punch out holes from both cardboard pieces with handheld hole punch. Use cardboard as template on top of paper to mark binding holes. Square up paper, mark holes, and punch a few sheets of paper at a time until finished. Assemble book and line up book holes.

Place a button over book hole on front cover and place another button over same hole on back cover. Thread needle with elastic string. Starting from back cover button, insert needle into button hole, through book hole, and up through button hole on front cover. Leave a 3-inch tail of elastic string sticking out of back cover button to tie off string. Insert needle back down into front cover buttonhole through to the back buttonhole and continue until button is securely sewn. Cut excess string and tie off using 3-inch tail string. Repeat process with other buttons and remaining book hole.

Punch a hole in both front and back cover, ½ inch in from right margin at the margin midpoint. Feed ribbon or a shoelace through back cover hole and knot at ribbon midpoint. Use ribbon as fastener through front cover hole to keep book closed. Using pinking shears, cut a rectangular piece of decorative fabric that is smaller than front cover to frame photo. Use spray adhesive or glue stick to attach fabric to front cover. Center a Father and child or family photo on fabric and attach using spray adhesive along with decorative picture corners. Attach photos to book pages and write captions under each picture.

Mason Jars Full of Flowers and Food

Use Mason jars full of colorful food as serving ware as well as a centerpiece. Also, float a few stemmed flowers in Mason jars full of water to add to nature's beauty.

A Spirited

Independence Day

July 4, 1976

The Story of Independence Day

Life, liberty, and the pursuit of happiness are the reasons we celebrate this day of America's birth. Our Fourth of July holiday commemorates the signing of the Declaration of Independence by the Continental Congress in 1776. Still feeling the pressures and paying the taxes of the empire they left over one hundred years prior, those living in the thirteen colonies of the New World felt the need for independence. The document signed by our forefathers was essentially a declaration of treason, as they were still British citizens of a territory ruled by King George, III.

People in this new land that they had worked so hard to establish, with little help from the king, rebelled against a policy of "taxation without representation." In September 1774, the First Continental Congress met and drafted a list of complaints against the king. In 1775, the king, sensing civil unrest, sent British troops to Concord, Massachusetts, to take

JULY

National Ice Cream Month

National Piña Colada Day (July 10)

Take Your Plants for a Walk Day (July 27)

August

National Golf Month

Elvis Week (second week of August)

National Toasted Marshmallow Day (August 30)

care of the situation. This was the time of Paul Revere's fabled midnight ride, when he alerted all that "the British were coming." The ensuing battle sparked the beginning of the Revolutionary War, with George Washington taking command of the Continental Army.

Over the next year the congress and England tried to come up with a fair and peaceful solution, to no avail. In June 1776, a group of men decided to formalize a declaration. Thomas Jefferson would write the document and present it to congress for revision. On July 4, in Philadelphia, after all had had their say, a vote was taken. Two colonies, Pennsylvania and South Carolina, voted nay, Delaware was undecided, New York abstained, and nine colonies voted in favor of our Declaration of Independence. A boisterous John Hancock, president of the Second Continental Congress, signed the document with a larger-than-life signature, followed by the fathers of our country, Thomas Jefferson, Benjamin Franklin, and John Adams, to name a few of these fifty-six brave men.

The declaration was printed in newspapers and read publicly during the month of July, and its words met with triumphant approval and cheering colonists. The War of Independence continued until 1783. Over 150 years later, in 1941, Congress declared July Fourth a federal holiday. Every year since freedom was first declared in 1776, people have celebrated with firecrackers popping, bells ringing, and people proudly waving flags.

Festive Traditions and Folklore

A Fourth of July celebration always inspires a feeling of strength, unity, and patriotism in citizens of these United States of America. The ideal choice for our Independence Day bash was to relive the Bicentennial of 1976. This two-hundred-year birthday party for the USA made our country seem as if it was still in its toddler years compared with the rest of the world. As we basked in the afterglow of fireworks, we felt lucky to be able to live free, and remembered how recent it was that we were not.

The spirit of the seventies coincides humorously with the spirit that founded this country. The "me decade," pinned on the public by the media, was a time of social exploration and self-reflective thought. Fortunately, for all of us, people like George Washington and Thomas Jefferson were thinking of the "us generation" and our future.

The American Flag

Every July Fourth Old Glory waves atop flagpoles and on little sticks in children's hands. Back in 1776 when our forefathers were signing the Declaration of Independence, a committee was appointed to design a symbol for the United States of America. Although Betsy Ross sewed the first flag, it was designed by Continental Congress member Francis Hopkinson. In 1777, on June 14, which we celebrate as Flag Day, a flag of thirteen alternating red and white stripes containing a blue field in the corner with a ring of thirteen stars was accepted as a representation of our country. Contrary to popular opinion, the colors on the flag were not intended to have a specific meaning. Over the years people have respectively come to associate the white stripes with purity, the red stripes with courage, and the blue field with justice. The number of stars has always represented the number of states.

Fireworks

The patriotic "rockets' red glare" and "bombs bursting in air," fireworks exploding in the sky is the grand finale of every July Fourth celebration. This glorious display in the summer night reminds us of our first celebrations in 1776, when muskets were fired into the air resonating the sounds of a newly formed country. The story goes that in 1922, an Italian man, Constantino Vitale, came to America with a spectacular secret for making fireworks, and skyrockets have been soaring every Independence Day since then.

Uncle Sam

This political cartoon figure is a classic Independence Day figure. His initials, U.S., stand for United States. Sam's image was first seen on a

Astronauts in the *Columbia* shuttle shout "Happy Birthday America" from space in 1992.

Hirofumi Nakajima of Japan sets a new hot-dog-eating world record in 1997 by scarfing down twenty-four and a half Nathan's hot dogs in twelve minutes.

In 1997, the VivaVegie Organization pickets the hot-dog-eating contest shouting, "Give peas a chance. Go vegetarian!"

World War I recruitment poster designed by James Montgomery Flagg, with the slogan "I Want You." This stern-looking guy with top hat and pointed finger was later adopted as a national symbol in 1961.

The Star-Spangled Banner

In September 1814, poet Francis Scott Key wrote "The Star–Spangled Banner." The official anthem of the U.S.A. since 1931, this musical tribute tells the story of men fighting for our country at the battle of Fort McHenry in Baltimore, Maryland. After a perilous night at war, Francis Scott Key awoke and was awestruck by the flag still waving high and proud. His inspired words are sung on every political occasion and to kick off sporting events.

Patriotic Parades

Dust off the old fire engine and dress her up in red, white, and blue bunting. Neighborhood parades are a wonderful custom, with communities marching down the streets in celebration. Our favorite parts of the parade are the four guys, one always bandaged and limping, representing the fife-and-drum corps, and the dogs pulled in a little red wagon.

Bicentennial Barbecue for Twenty

A hallmark of American history, our celebrations on July 4, 1976, gave the country a real reason to feast. Barbecues were fired up all over the nation in anticipation of the first fireworks. What better way to capture the spirit of our forefathers and excitement of the bicentennial than with spicy fare for this customarily outdoor event.

There are no real food traditions when it comes to this holiday, but it seems everyone has a favorite dish that they make. Of course one item has to be red, white, and blue, typically the dessert. As the seventies was a decade of "free thinking," Americans began tinkering with everything from their inner selves to their recipes. People's idea of epicurean expression was different than in times past. Vegetarianism came to light with the 1971 opening of Alice Waters's restaurant Chez Panisse in California. Ironically, the health-food craze occurred just before a couple of guys in Vermont, Ben and Jerry, renovated a gas station in 1978 into a luxurious ice-cream mecca. It was a decade of revolution, from the palate to personal fulfillment.

Papaya, Jicama, and Red Onion Slaw in Blueberry Vinaigrette

Zesty Potato and Black Bean Salad

Spicy and Sweet Barbecue-Sauced Pork Ribs

Lemonade and blended fruit drinks

Watermelon Caramel Flan

Papaya, Jicama, and Red Onion Slaw in Blueberry Vinaigrette

Bing! Bam! Boom! Coleslaw that will knock your socks off and shoot bursts of color is a must on your Fourth of July table.

1 cup fresh blueberries, rinsed

1/4 cup white grape juice

2 tablespoons white wine vinegar

1 cup canola oil

1/4 teaspoon salt

1/2 teaspoon sugar

2 large heads red cabbage, finely shredded

1 medium jicama, peeled, coarsely grated (see Note below)

2 papayas, peeled, seeded, cut into small cubes (about 5 cups)

1 medium red onion, cut into slivers

MAKES 20 SERVINGS

Place blueberries in a large bowl and crush with the back of a spoon. Add grape juice, vinegar, oil, salt, and sugar, and whisk together until combined. Cover with plastic wrap and let stand at room temperature overnight.

NOTE Jicama is a vegetable with a crisp white interior and a rough brown skin. Peel off the skin before slicing. It is similar in texture to an apple.

Combine cabbage, jicama, papayas, and onion in a large bowl. Pour vinaigrette over cabbage mixture and toss to combine. (It may be necessary to divide mixture between 2 bowls for tossing.)

Serve cool or at room temperature. (Store covered in plastic wrap in the refrigerator up to 2 days.)

Zesty Potato and Black Bean Salad

Yep! We've added black beans to this barbecue favorite, giving it festive flecks with a Baja lime flavoring.

8 pounds russet potatoes, peeled, cut into 1-inch cubes

1 tablespoon plus 1 teaspoon salt

2 cloves garlic, minced

1 tablespoon whole coriander seeds, crushed

2 tablespoons minced pimientos

$\frac{1}{3}$ cup white wine vinegar

$\frac{1}{3}$ cup fresh lime juice

$\frac{3}{4}$ cup olive oil

$\frac{1}{2}$ teaspoon black pepper

2 (15-ounce) cans black beans, rinsed, drained

MAKES 20 SERVINGS

Place potatoes and 1 tablespoon salt in a large stockpot and cover with water. Bring to a boil over medium-high heat and cook until tender, about 20 minutes. Drain in colander and transfer to a large bowl.

Meanwhile, whisk together garlic, coriander, pimientos, vinegar, lime juice, oil, 1 teaspoon salt, and pepper until combined.

Add black beans and lime juice mixture to potatoes. Toss gently to avoid mashing potatoes, until combined. Serve at room temperature. (Store covered in plastic wrap in the refrigerator up to 2 days.)

Spicy and Sweet Barbecue-Sauced Pork Ribs

Making a batch of rich, mahogany-colored barbecue sauce is serious business. Although this menu has a Latin influence, we've thrown a curveball into the mix by sweetening it with an Asian hoisin sauce. You can parboil ribs in water as we've suggested—this will save time on the grill—or slap these baby backs on a low flame and baste for hours until done.

20 pounds baby-back pork loin spareribs or 20 chicken fryer pieces

SPICY AND SWEET BARBECUE SAUCE
2 cups water

2 tablespoons hoisin sauce

3 tablespoons light brown sugar

1 teaspoon salt

1 teaspoon black pepper

1 teaspoon cayenne pepper

2 tablespoons chili powder

2 cloves garlic, minced

¼ cup Worcestershire sauce

4 cups ketchup

1 teaspoon Liquid Smoke

MAKES 20 SERVINGS

Place ribs in several large stockpots. Add enough water to each pot so that the ribs are covered. Parboil ribs by bringing liquid to a boil over high heat. Then reduce heat to low, cover, and simmer 1 hour. Remove ribs from pot and drain off liquid. (If using chicken, it does not need to be boiled before grilling.)

To make barbecue sauce: Combine all ingredients in a large pot. Bring to boil over medium-high heat. Reduce heat and simmer uncovered, stirring occasionally, until sauce thickens, 20 minutes. Cool to room temperature to allow flavors to blend.

Heat gas barbecue according to manufacturer's instructions for low heat or follow instructions on charcoal bag for low coals. Set grill rack about 6 inches above coals and place parboiled ribs on grill. Brush sauce over ribs and grill, turning ribs over and basting with sauce every 10 minutes, until tender and browned, about 20 minutes. Ribs will be done when the meat separates from the bone about ½ inch on the ends; also, rib backing often cracks. (If cooking chicken, grill for about 30 minutes, turning occasionally. Brush with sauce and grill until cooked through, about 15 minutes, removing smaller pieces as they finish.)

NOTE Hoisin sauce can be found in the Asian section of grocery stores.

Place racks on a serving platter or cut ribs in between bones for individual portions and serve.

Watermelon Caramel Flan

Jolly Rancher watermelon candy has such a yummy and refreshing flavor that we couldn't resist experimenting with it in a caramel for flan. The results are amazing!

1 cup sugar

3 tablespoons water

8 (18-gram) pieces Jolly Rancher watermelon hard candy

8 eggs

1½ cups heavy cream

1½ cups milk

1 teaspoon pure vanilla extract

2 cups sliced fresh strawberries

½ cup fresh blueberries

MAKES 15 TO 20 SERVINGS

Combine ½ cup of the sugar, water, and candy in a small saucepan. Bring to a boil over high heat and boil without stirring until candy has melted, the mixture deepens in color, and you smell a watermelon scent, 3 to 5 minutes. Watch carefully to avoid burning. Remove from heat and pour hot caramel into a 10-inch round pan, tilting pan to coat bottom of pan with caramel. Set aside.

Preheat oven to 325F (165C). Beat eggs and remaining ½ cup sugar until thick and pale yellow. Add cream, milk, and vanilla and beat until blended.

Pour flan mixture into caramel-lined pan. Place round pan in a slightly larger pan. Pour enough hot water in larger pan to reach halfway up sides of cake pan. Bake about 2 hours, or until flan appears set and a knife inserted off center comes out clean. Carefully remove flan from oven to avoid spilling the hot water. Remove flan pan from water bath and cool completely. Cover with plastic wrap and refrigerate overnight.

Place a inverted a large, flat serving platter on top of flan pan. Holding the platter and the pan, flip over onto platter. Remove pan and and wipe off excess liquid from sides. (Because candy is used in the caramel, it contains more liquid than usual.)

Just before serving, arrange blueberries and strawberries in a patriotic pattern on top of flan. Serve cool. (Store covered in the refrigerator up to 1 week.)

Independence Day Decor and Personal Touches

Cool Red, White, and Blue Light-Up Banners

For each banner, buy the following:

> FROM FABRIC STORE: 4 yards of red, white, or blue cotton satin fabric for banner; 1 yard patriotic color fabric for wrapping
>
> FROM HARDWARE STORE: 1 bright lantern flashlight; 1 (10-inch-diameter) plastic plant container; 45-inch length (1-inch-diameter) plastic PVC pipe; 1 yard double-stick carpet tape; (optional) fishing line
>
> FROM CRAFT OR PARTY STORE: gold metallic stars

These vertical banners hang from a roof or gutter and taper down to the ground. Determine where you will install the banner and measure the height from roof to ground. Add 24 inches to the measured height to determine the length of banner fabric. Roll up 8 inches of fabric, starting from one end, onto PVC pipe and adhere roll to fabric with strip of double-stick carpet tape. Place pipe in gutter and weight down with a small rock on either end, obviously do not use heavy rocks that will damage your gutter! Or string fishing line through PVC pipe and hang from roof by your own method just as you hang Christmas lights.

Place the plant container on ground behind the banner. Tuck bottom of banner fabric under planter and place a few rocks in planter to weight down. Wrap patriotic fabric around end of banner and planter. Tie fabric at back of planter or secure with pins for finished look. Place flashlight in plant container with light shining up and toward back of banner. Adhere gold stars to front of banner using double-stick tape. These banners are great for decor during the daytime and will have an illuminating effect at night while watching fireworks.

Opposite page:
Patriotic lighted banners
decorate the party.

Fireworks Drinking Glasses

FROM HARDWARE STORE: 1 yard per glass of 12-gauge, colored solid insulated wire (a color for each glass)

Wrap wire up stems of wine, margarita, or martini glasses. Continue a spiraling wire around bowl of glass. Bend wire at top rim of glass into a fun shape that will extend above rim of glass. Using wire cutters, trim excess wire so end is safe and does not stick out. Great shapes are orange wire spirals, red wire hearts, or yellow wire stars. These are not only fun but they are also a good way to keep track of everyone's drink.

Starred Blue Bowl with Red and White Carnations

For each centerpiece, purchase the following:

FROM OFFICE SUPPLY STORE: 1 pack gold star stickers like the teacher used to award

FROM FABRIC STORE: 1 (24 × 15-inch) rectangle of blue satin fabric

FROM FLORIST: 8-inch-wide glass bubble bowl; 5 white carnations; 10 red carnations

Lay blue satin rectangle, right side down, and lay bubble wrap in the center of satin with long sides running the same way. Lay a 4-inch-high clear drinking glass on its side at a 12-inch end of bubble wrap, centering glass in middle of wrap. Loosely roll up glass in both satin and bubble wrap (similar to candy rolled in a wrapper). Turn rolled glass so open end is upright. Lower the rolled glass into bubble bowl. Fold under top edges of fabric and bubble wrap around glass to neaten. Smooth fabric from within bowl so bubble wrap and raw edges of fabric are not visible from exterior of bowl.

Patriotic Spirit Wagon

Fill a red wagon with party supplies for guests to decorate themselves. Include temporary tattoos of flags; red, white, and blue clown wigs; sunglasses; and face paints.

Opposite page:
Unique fireworks glasses and a bubble bowl filled
with red, white, and blue make a festive Fourth.

A Happy Halloween

October 31, 1950

The Story of Halloween

Over two-thousand years ago in what we now know as Ireland, the druids marked the end of summer or *samhain* (sow-in) with a celebration. This November 1 gala rang in their new year and paid homage to their sun god in hopes that the coming winter would not be too severe. On the eve of October 31, they believed that the dead came back to the earth. They would dampen their hearth fires, making their homes uninviting to spirits, and don costumes to disguise themselves from the dead. At the celebration, huge bonfires were lit and sacrifices made to appease the spirits. Although the druids feared the entities, they felt that their "presence" opened them up to the powers of the "other world," and that the supernatural connection would help predict the future in the bleak months ahead.

In southern Italy, the Romans also held a harvest festival. They honored Pomona, the goddess of fruit trees. By A.D. 43, the Romans had conquered most of the Celtic territory. Under Roman rule, samhain and the festival of Pomona blended together, along with *feralia,* a late-October celebration in which the Romans remembered those who had passed away.

SEPTEMBER
National Good Manners Month

Substitute Teacher Appreciation Week (second full week of September)

One Hit Wonder Appreciation Day (September 25)

OCTOBER
National Roller Skating Month

National Pet Peeve Week (second full week of October)

National Bring Your Teddy Bear to Work Day (second Wednesday in October)

Christianity was practiced in many Celtic lands by the seventh century, and Pope Boniface IV adopted the pagan celebrations and named them All Saints' Day, in honor of saints and martyrs. The name Halloween was derived from "hallow," an old English term meaning to sanctify and "all-hallowmas," meaning All Saints' Day. Since the celebration was in the evening, the title eventually changed to All Hallow's Eve.

It is believed that the Scottish and Irish brought the traditions of Halloween to America in the nineteenth century. Halloween had become a secular holiday by 1920. The new focus was on family, and people attempted to strip the dark elements from the day. Townships would host parties with parades and entertainment. However, mischief makers used this spooky celebration as an opportunity to vandalize. Parents and civic leaders worked hard to preserve the family nature of this holiday. One solution was to give kids a "treat" so they would not play any "tricks" on the community. By 1950, Halloween had become the neighborly night of costumes and candy that we know today. One of the world's oldest holidays, Halloween is still celebrated in many countries.

Festive Traditions and Folklore

One of the happiest holidays for children, Halloween's origins are full of ritual and mysticism. We chose to set Halloween in a time when the holiday was at its wholesome best! On Halloween in 1950, the Trick-or-Treat for UNICEF program started when a Sunday-school class decided to collect coins for needy children instead of asking for candy. This custom continues today with more than two million young ambassadors each year who have raised over $100 million for the poor. Now, we don't advocate trading in the candy collecting for quarters, but the combination of the two traditions is pretty sweet.

Although we've tagged this holiday for the kids, many adults celebrate, too, and relive childhood memories through their children's antics and giving candy at the door. The "big kids" also have a blast decorating the house and creating the ultimate spine-chilling mood. Many strange customs and bits of Halloween folklore have come and gone over time.

Here are some of our favorites for you to mix and match at your next frightful bash.

Trick-or-Treating

Few haven't experienced the joy of this tradition, where children dressed in costume go door-to-door in hopes of receiving candy. They must say "trick or treat" before a sweet is dropped into their pillowcases, plastic jack-o'-lanterns, or any container that can hold a load of candy.

There are differing theories on how the practice of trick-or-treating came to be. Some think it sprang up from good intentions, because a sense of community was gained as kids ran from one house to the next in the neighborhood. Others think that it began as a peace offering of a little candy to keep vandals from acting up. In actuality, it probably was a holdover from the old tradition of "going a-souling." When English children would "go a-souling," they traveled door-to-door begging for soul cakes, somewhat similar to scones or cookies. People gave them cakes to ward off spirits and in exchange for prayers for their dearly departed.

Dressing in Costume

This tradition has a few twists and turns. Many cultures believed that the spirits of the departed returned to visit their earthly homes during Halloween. People left food out for the spirits as well as chairs so they could rest. This old tradition evolved into people masquerading as departed spirits and going door-to-door, begging for treats. Also, the druids disguised themselves during their festivals, which may be considered the very first Halloween costumes.

Wearing Masks

Initially, masks warded off evil spirits and hid one's identity. Folklore suggests that members of upper society and even nobles liked to attend witch sabbaths. These rites were not considered proper for members of their station, so they disguised themselves with masks. Also, some

Americans purchase twenty million pounds of candy corn in 1999. The American Dental Association is likely disturbed by this statistic.

Dave Stelts of Leetonia, Ohio, breaks the world record for growing the largest pumpkin in the year 2000. His giant gourd weighs 1,140 pounds, exceeding the previous record by nine pounds.

By 2001, Halloween is the number-one candy-consuming holiday in America. The National Confectioners' Association projects sales of $2,035 billion. Nationwide, trick-or-treaters continue to be disappointed when well-meaning families place apples in their bags in lieu of refined-sugar products.

In 1450, the first major witch-hunts begin throughout Europe.

believe that wearing a mask on Halloween will bring good luck in the coming year. In Ireland, it was believed that Muck Olla, a druidic god, would wreak havoc on crops and farms if he was not honored. Priests would don masks and go house to house for cakes, collecting the farmer's "dues" and keeping the farm from harm.

Jack-O'-Lanterns

Irish folklore gives us the tradition of the jack-o'-lantern. According to legend, a man named Jack was a prankster and drunkard. He tricked the devil into climbing a tree and trapped him up there by carving a cross in the trunk. Jack struck a deal with Satan; in order to be free from the tree he must never tempt him again. When Jack died, he was not allowed into heaven or hell because of the notorious deal. The devil gave Jack one ember to light his way through eternal darkness. Jack put the ember inside a hollowed-out turnip to keep it burning as long as possible. The Irish originally used turnips as their jack-o'-lanterns, but upon coming to America, they found that pumpkins were more plentiful.

Witches and Ghosts

Many of these eerie figures have pagan roots. The word *witch* comes from the Saxon word *wica* or wise one. According to ancient literature, Halloween, sometimes called the witches' sabbath, is a time for dancing and feasting. Ghosts are symbolic of the dead, who the druids believed walked the earth during the samhain festival.

Bobbing for Apples

The tradition of apple games at Halloween celebrations has been tied to the fall harvest and the ancient Roman festival honoring Pomona, goddess of the fruit tree. Apples are placed in a tub, made from wood in olden days and zinc today. The tub is filled halfway with water. One person stirs the water as another tries to bite the moving apples. Some say that the game is competitive and the winner is the one who catches the most apples. Others bob for the fun of it!

Halloween Dessert Party for Sixteen

There is only one food rule for Halloween . . . lots of sugar. In the fifties, along with the first UNICEF funds collected, trick-or-treaters were also tallying up candy bars. By this decade, the Hershey bar had been around since 1894, along with now-century-old sweets including Clark bars (1886), Good & Plenty (1893), Tootsie Rolls (1896), and Cracker Jacks (1893). The following years leading up to this wholesome era also gave us LifeSavers (1912) Milk Duds (1928), York Peppermint Patties (1940), and M&M's, Jolly Ranchers, Junior Mints, and Whoppers (1941). History is full of sweets!

Although this Halloween party menu may favor an adult's taste buds, a fright night celebration isn't complete unless chocolate bugs and gory edibles creep onto the buffet table. We've conjured some fun creepy nibblers for your party as well as a recipe for soul cakes, which ties in to the ancient ritual known as "going a-souling."

Spiced Soul Cakes

Red Caramel Fondue

Pumpkin Cream Dip

Fruits and Cookies, For Dipping

Creepy Nibblers

Blackberry and Pear Mulled Cider

Spiced Soul Cakes

English children collected soul cakes as they went door-to-door on All Hallows' Eve. Our shortbread take on these treats of yore will taste divine drizzled with Red Caramel Fondue (see below).

2 sticks (1 cup) unsalted butter, softened

1/2 cup packed plus 3 tablespoons

1/4 cup powdered sugar

2 cups all-purpose flour

1/2 teaspoon fresh grated nutmeg

1 teaspoon ground cinnamon

1/2 teaspoon ground ginger

MAKES ABOUT 24 COOKIES

Preheat oven to 325F (165C). Spray 2 baking sheets with a very light coat of nonstick cooking spray. Add butter to a mixing bowl and whip until creamy. Add 1/2 cup brown sugar and powdered sugar and beat until fluffy. Sift together dry ingredients and knead into mixture until thoroughly combined.

Form balls from 1 tablespoon of dough and flatten into 1/4-inch-thick rounds. Or roll out dough onto a floured surface to 1/4-inch thickness and cut out Halloween shapes using cookie cutters. Place cookies on prepared baking sheets.

Bake for 20 to 25 minutes, or until edges are browned. Transfer to a wire rack. Sprinkle the 3 tablespoons brown sugar over top of hot cookies.

(Store in an airtight container for up to 1 week at room temperature.)

Red Caramel Fondue

There's nothing like the taste of homemade caramel, and with a little splash of red food coloring, this sauce gets a Halloween makeover. Use caution and a great big pot when making this sauce, as it will spatter when the cream is added.

2 cups sugar

2 cups heavy cream

10 drops red food coloring

SUGGESTED ITEMS FOR DIPPING
Apple wedges, pear wedges, pineapple cubes, banana slices, strawberries, cherries (pitted), melon cubes, Spiced Soul Cakes (above), cubed pound cake, biscotti, pretzels

MAKES ABOUT 3 CUPS

Heat sugar in a medium saucepan over medium-high heat. Cook, stirring occasionally with a long wooden spoon, until sugar dissolves and turns into a golden amber color. If the sugar seems to be turning from amber to dark brown too quickly, reduce heat to medium-low as it might burn.

Reduce heat to medium-low and add cream carefully as the mixture will spatter. Cook, stirring constantly with long wooden spoon, until mixture is smooth, about 10 minutes. Reduce heat to low and simmer 5 minutes. Test caramel by adding a small drop to cold water; if caramel sinks to the bottom, it is ready. If caramel does not sink, continue to cook, testing every 2 minutes, until ready. Remove from heat and stir in food coloring until caramel is a scary red color.

Transfer to a fondue pot over a low flame. Arrange fruit and dipping items on a platter or in small bowls and serve alongside fondue. (Store any leftover fondue covered in the refrigerator.)

NOTES The fondue can be made a couple of days before use if covered in an airtight container and refrigerated. Warm fondue in a double boiler or small saucepan set over a simmering pot of water just before serving.

Fruit should be cut just before serving and refrigerated until needed. Lightly brush cut apples, pears, and bananas with lemon juice to keep from browning as long as possible. Set these items on the buffet table in small amounts at a time for maximum freshness.

Pumpkin Cream Dip

We humorously refer to the fifties as the "dip decade." The classic onion soup mix and sour cream dip along with clam dip were born in this era. Strawberries are excellent with Pumpkin Cream Dip. For more ideas, see Items for Dipping under Red Caramel Fondue (page 100).

2 tablespoons unsalted butter

1 (15-ounce) can pureed pumpkin pulp

3 tablespoons light brown sugar

2 cups sour cream

1 small pumpkin, seeds and strings removed

MAKES ABOUT 3 CUPS

Melt butter in a large skillet over medium heat. Add pumpkin and brown sugar and cook pumpkin, stirring occasionally, 8 to 10 minutes. Remove from heat and cool to room temperature.

Place sour cream in a large bowl. Stir in pumpkin mixture until combined. Cover with plastic wrap and refrigerate until ready to serve. Spoon into hollowed pumpkin and serve cool. (Do not keep dip that has been unrefrigerated for more than 30 minutes.)

Creepy Nibblers

A Halloween table isn't complete unless a few gory tidbits are served.

Gummy Worms in Lady Apples

Wash and dry the Lady Apples. Bore 2 holes in apple with a corkscrew and insert gummy worms in holes.

Eyeballs

Hard-cook eggs, cool, and peel. Slice each egg in half crosswise and remove the yolk. Place the white egg halves, cut sides down, and use the rounded side as the whites of eyes. Place cooked yolks in a small bowl and mix in green or blue food coloring. Buy a new paintbrush; do not use a paintbrush that has been used with actual, nonedible paint. Use the brush to paint the iris of the eye on each egg white half with colored yolks. Slice the tip off a black olive and place in center of iris for eye's pupil.

Witch Hat

Ice a cookie with chocolate frosting. Place a Hershey's Kiss in the cookie's center.

Fudge Spiders with Black Licorice Legs

Form chocolate fudge into round balls for spider bodies. Cut black licorice Twizzlers into thin strips about 1 inch long. Insert licorice strips in fudge balls for spider legs.

Blackberry and Pear Mulled Cider

A warm witches' brew, this version is for the kiddies after a long night of trick-or-treating. Elders may prefer to add a little Halloween spirit to their mulled cider by lacing it with rum or spiced brandy.

1 gallon apple cider

1 cup fresh or frozen blackberries

2 Bartlett pears, washed, cut into wedges

4 cinnamon sticks

1 teaspoon ground ginger

MAKES ABOUT 1 GALLON

Place cider, blackberries, pears, cinnamon sticks, and ginger in a large pot. Bring to a boil over medium-high heat. Reduce heat to low and simmer, uncovered, for 30 minutes.

Using a slotted spoon, remove blackberries and cinnamon sticks. Keep cider in pot over low flame on stove for guests to help themselves. Or place cider in round chafer over low flame with ladle and mugs nearby on buffet table.

NOTE Why are we removing the blackberries and not the pears? The blackberries lose their color and turn an unappetizing gray after being cooked in the cider.

Spooky Trees

For 2 trees:

> FROM HARDWARE STORE: 1 (10 × 4-foot) roll black mesh fiberglass screening; plastic sheeting; 1 (10 × 4-foot-wide) roll aviary or chicken wire; 12 feet of 14-gauge metal wire; 20 feet of 22-gauge metal wire; 2 (10-inch-diameter) plastic plant containers; 2 bright lantern flashlights; duct tape
>
> FROM CRAFT STORE: white glue and assorted colors of glitter

Using scissors, cut the mesh into 2 pieces: a 4 × 4-foot piece and a 6 × 4-foot piece. Cut a jagged edge on a 4-foot side of each mesh piece for top of tree. Lay mesh pieces flat on a surface that is covered with plastic sheeting. Decorate the tree with glue and glitter by making scary faces, knot holes, bark lines, and a sparkling jagged edge at the top. Allow glue to dry completely.

Using wire cutters and wearing protective gloves, cut the chicken wire into 2 pieces: a 4 × 4-foot piece and a 6 × 4-foot long piece. Also, cut 12 (1-foot) pieces from the 14-gauge wire. Bend wire pieces into a hairpin shape to be used as anchors to secure the tree into the ground. Bend chicken wire into 2 columns: a 4-foot-high column and a 6-foot-high column. Insert pieces of 22-gauge wire through chicken wire and twist-tie to keep column closed along back seam. Bend all chicken wire ends in and under at top to make edges safe and for a neater look.

Place plant containers on lawn where spooky trees will be located. Set columns around containers. Anchor columns by inserting 14-gauge wire hairpins into chicken wire and ground around column bottom. Wrap decorated mesh around wire columns. Temporarily secure mesh back seam with duct tape. Secure mesh to chicken wire by weaving 22-gauge wire up along back seam; remove tape. At night, lower lit flashlights down into plant containers with string or wire line through top of tree. Make sure light is shining up to illuminate glittered features. (NOT RECOMMENDED FOR WINDY OR RAINY WEATHER.)

Jack-O'-Color Lanterns

For 4 pumpkins, buy the following:

FROM LIGHTING STORE OR LOCAL SCHOOL THEATER DEPARTMENT: 4 (12-inch-square) colored lighting gels, a different color for each pumpkin; 1 (100-foot) strand miniature white Christmas lights with blinking effects

FROM HARDWARE STORE: duct tape

FROM SUPERMARKET OR FARMERS MARKET: 4 large pumpkins in assorted sizes

FROM PARTY OR CRAFT: polyester cobwebs

Cut around each pumpkin stem, making a lid in top of each pumpkin. Remove seeds and pulp from inside. Carve out the facial features using a small cutting knife. Cut a 1-inch-diameter hole on pumpkin's opposite side from face. Cut lighting gel sheet into a rectangle that is large enough to fit inside of pumpkin behind face. Place gel inside pumpkin, flat against back side of face. From inside of pumpkin, insert wooden picks through gel into pumpkin to keep gel in place; insert a pick in each corner of gel and wherever necessary around gel perimeter. Feed 1-foot portion of miniature lights strand through hole in back of pumpkin. For many pumpkins side by side continue feeding 1-foot portions of light strand into backs of pumpkins, allowing for strand slack in between pumpkins. Plug light cord into an electrical outlet, using extension cord if necessary. Using duct tape, tape down any cords that may be in trick-or-treaters' pathway. Do not use candles with lighting gels, because the gels will melt. Drape cobwebs over the pumpkins.

Opposite page:
Cobweb-covered jack-o'-lanterns are
displayed on hay bales.

A Victorious Thanksgiving

November 23, 1944

The Story of Thanksgiving

Most of us know the story of this holiday from an elementary-school play in which we were donned Pilgrim hats or feathers, acting out the first Thanksgiving feast. In the seventeenth century, our Pilgrim fathers set sail on the *Mayflower* in search of a happier way of life and religious freedom. They landed at Plymouth Rock in Massachusetts in 1620. Ironically, there is no reference to the actual rock as a landing place in the Pilgrims' accounts, but they do cite the famed piece of granite in writings about a hundred years later.

The first winter in Plymouth was severe and many Pilgrims lost their lives. Seeing the hardships of these struggling people, the Native Americans befriended the Pilgrims and taught them the way of the land. Squanto, as he was called by the Pilgrims, and others from his tribe showed the newcomers how to plant corn and squash and to hunt and fish. As a result of working together the harvest was bountiful. A feast was held to give thanks for the gifts of the land and the kindness of the Native Americans.

The actual date of the first Thanksgiving is unknown. In later years,

Benjamin Franklin, in a 1784 letter to his daughter, suggests that the turkey is a more "respectable" symbol of the United States than the "lazy" bald eagle.

NOVEMBER

Peanut Butter Lovers' Month

Random Acts of Kindness Week (November 11 to 17)

National Sandwich Day (November 3)

In 1816, the first harvest of cultivated cranberries is recorded, in Cape Cod, Massachusetts. If only those early farmers could have known that their labors would one day lead to Cran-Mango Cocktail.

In 1947, the National Turkey Federation begins its annual presentation of a live turkey to the president of the United States. With the president "pardoning" the poultry, this becomes an annual ritual that announces the Thanksgiving season and a media frenzy for years to come.

In 1999, about 273 million turkeys are eaten in America, 45 million of them on Thanksgiving Day.

the Pilgrims feasted only when the harvest was plentiful. During the next century, records indicate that the handful of people who populated the land had some sort of fall celebration. George Washington wished to establish Thanksgiving as a holiday on November 26, 1789, but with all the political turmoil of the day, the feast never made it into the records. In 1863, Abraham Lincoln proclaimed the last Thursday in November to be Thanksgiving Day. But, it wasn't until 1941 that President Roosevelt signed a bill that designated the fourth Thursday as the national holiday. However, each year the President must still proclaim the official date of Thanksgiving.

Some hold hands in silent prayer, while others express gratitude aloud, but all gather around the table and give thanks for what they have.

Festive Traditions and Folklore

By Thanksgiving 1944, Americans were harvesting their Victory Gardens in anticipation of a bountiful holiday. Newsreels projected the image of a wartime country in which canned goods were being rationed and Americans were called upon to do their part at home. Economic hardship led to agricultural growth and 20 million people planted gardens, which produced 40 percent of the nation's food. For many, gardening became a family event or community activity, bringing people together during this tumultuous era. If ever Thanksgiving was a time to be grateful for what one had and appreciate time spent with loved ones, it was then.

Most of this holiday's traditions are centered on food and football! Families have developed their own traditions to stave off their appetites as the smell of turkey fills the house. As the bird is being carved, everyone comes together to feast and to fill their hearts with thanks.

Turkey and the Trimmings

Surprisingly, there is no real evidence of turkey being served at the first Thanksgiving feasts in the early seventeenth century. Apparently, "turkey" was the generic name to describe all fowl. Venison pops up in many historical accounts of the holiday as well as corn, boiled pumpkin, berries, and even shellfish. Most families still include pumpkin as the traditional pie, and berries are represented in cranberry sauce.

Indian Corn

Hanging multicolored corn with husks attached on our doors is a custom that reminds us how important corn was to the survival of early colonists. Native Americans, who helped the Pilgrims plant corn, believed the grain to be divine. Many ancient cultures celebrated the fall harvest by honoring gods of corn and grain, including the Greek goddess Demeter and the Roman goddess Ceres.

Macy's Thanksgiving Day Parade

Just about every American turns on the television to see the enormous floating balloons in the Macy's Thanksgiving Day parade. Since 1927, New Yorkers flock to the streets to see grand characters fly through the air, and many gather the night before to watch the process of inflating the balloons.

Thanksgiving Day Football

For some people, a holiday when football is the focus is their most prized of all. In 1874, the first intercollegiate football game was played. Soon after, the Northeast Intercollegiate Football Association was formed with its championship game scheduled to take place on Thanksgiving Day. Since the late nineteenth century, Princeton and Yale have played each other almost every year on this day. The tradition caught on quickly and today many college and pro teams spend the day on the gridiron and their fans spend the day in front of the tube.

In Hawaii, King Kamehameha III and his queen celebrate their first Thanksgiving in 1849. Poi, a porridge made from taro root, is served luau style. The New Englanders who attend this celebration will remember it as the only Thanksgiving dinner at which they left the table hungry.

Jet-puffed marshmallows, their name derived from the process of infusing air into the candy during production, are first sold in 1953. Sweet potato casseroles will never be the same.

Vincent Pilkington of Dublin, Ireland, enters the *Guinness Book of World Records* in 1980 as the world's fastest turkey plucker. His record time is one minute and thirty seconds, beating his previous record.

Thanksgiving Feast for Twelve

Turkey is at the heart of most modern Thanksgiving feasts. A holiday full of traditional fare, stuffing, sweet potatoes, cranberries, and pumpkin pie also make an appearance on many tables across the country.

Our friends around the country have many methods of cooking turkey for a Thanksgiving feast. Dick Bartlett, who lives in New Hampshire, doesn't let the cold weather stop him from grilling the bird outdoors. Last year some Los Angeles friends tried a process called the "Mississippi trash bag method" in which the turkey soaks in a bag of brine before cooking to ensure a moister bird. And then there's the Southern deep-fried turkey; those who've used this technique swear by it! No matter how you enjoy your bird or whatever overflows from the cornucopia on your table, we know that you'll be celebrating with friends and family.

Sage and Cedar-Smoked Turkey on the Grill

Roasted Harvest Vegetables and Toasted Tarragon Stuffing

Molasses Sweet Potato Whip

Steamed Broccoli

Warm Cranberry Compote with Walnut Streusel Topping

Cran-apple punch

Pecan-Pumpkin Pie

Sage and Cedar-Smoked Turkey on the Grill

Many love Thanksgiving turkey cooked on the grill, despite the chilly temperatures in some states. We figure that you know how to cook a stuffed turkey in the oven and most birds have cooking instructions right on the manufacturer's bag. Here's a smoky alternative for the star of your feast.

1 (18- to 20-pound) turkey

SOAKING BRINE
6 quarts water

1 cup salt

2 large turkey-size oven bags (see Note below)

SAGE AND CEDAR CHIP FOIL BAGS
8 cups hickory-smoked chips, soaked in water 30 minutes, drained

4 cups whole fresh sage leaves, soaked in water 30 minutes, drained

8 heavy-duty oven foil bags

GLAZE
1/2 cup olive oil

2 tablespoons finely chopped fresh sage

2 tablespoons fresh lemon juice

1/4 cup fresh orange juice

1 teaspoon salt

1/2 teaspoon black pepper

MAKES 12 SERVINGS

If turkey is frozen, thaw overnight in refrigerator or in cold water.

Remove plastic wrapping on turkey. Remove neck and bag of giblets from body cavities. Rinse turkey, including cavities, thoroughly.

To make brine: Mix together water and salt in a large clean container. Double turkey-size oven bags and place turkey inside. Pour brine over turkey in bag and knot open end of bag to close. Place bagged turkey in large roasting pan to catch any leakage. Refrigerate at least 4 hours.

To make foil bags: Place 1 cup hickory chips plus 1/2 cup sage in each foil bag and fold ends to make a small pouch. Poke holes in top of pouch with a fork.

Preheat grill (see instructions for preparing charcoal, gas, or electric grill below).

Remove turkey from brine bag. Pat outer surface of turkey dry with paper towels. Rub olive oil over turkey skin. Insert a meat thermometer into thickest part of thigh without touching the bone.

Place unstuffed turkey, breast side up, on top cooking rack of grill, centered over the broiler drip pan. (For best results, turkey must fit under grill lid with at least 1 inch of space between turkey and lid.) Place foil pouches on either side of turkey. Cover grill, leaving vents open. Cook until thermometer registers 160F (70C). Every hour during cooking process replace both foil pouches with fresh pouches using long tongs and oven mitts. Add more water to drip pan as needed.

Meanwhile, to make glaze: Whisk together oil, sage, lemon juice, orange juice, salt, and pepper.

When meat thermometer is at 160F (70C), brush glaze mixture over entire surface of turkey. Cover grill and cook until thermometer registers 180F (80C), about 60 minutes longer. Cover any areas of turkey that are browning too quickly with foil.

Remove turkey from grill and let stand for 15 minutes, loosely tented with foil, before carving. To carve, cut off drumsticks and then wings at joints. Carve each breast on the diagonal and arrange turkey on a large platter and serve. (Store covered in plastic wrap in the refrigerator for up to 2 days.)

Charcoal Grill Preparation

Remove top cooking rack and open all vents. Mound about 40 briquettes in grill. Heat the briquettes until covered with gray ash, about 30 minutes. Using tongs, divide briquettes into 2 piles, about 8 inches apart. Place clean broiler pan containing 1/4 cup water between piles under center of cooking rack to catch drippings. Briquettes should be along both lengthwise sides of broiler pan. Place a foil pouch on rack above each pile of briquettes. Place cooking rack in grill 6 inches above coals. (Using a rack with handles along with long tongs and oven mitts makes it easier to replace foil pouches during cooking.) During cooking process add 6 to 10 briquettes to each side every hour along with foil pouches and add more charcoal to maintain a grill temperature near 325F (165C).

Gas or Electric Grill preparation

Preheat grill with all burners on high. Turn off center burner and lower outside burners to medium-low heat. Place foil pouches on rack over 2 lit outside burners. Place a clean broiler pan containing 1/4 cup water over the unlit center burner to catch drippings. Position the cooking rack at least 6 inches above burners.

NOTES If you choose to stuff your bird, allow about 2 hours more for cooking. Always refer to the meat thermometer, which will register 180F (80C) when your bird is done. The center of the stuffing should be 160F (70C).

When turkey is cooked on a covered grill, there may be a narrow rosy-pink band of meat just under the skin. This is due to charcoal combustion reacting with the meat pigment. This is not a sign of undercooked meat. Weather conditions such as colder temperatures, wind, and humidity may influence the cooking time. Place an oven thermometer in the appropriate place for your grill to monitor the temperature. It may be necessary to adjust the number of briquettes or the controls on a gas grill to maintain a constant temperature of 325F (165C).

Roasted Harvest Vegetables and Toasted Tarragon Stuffing

What a thrill it is to prepare vegetables from your own garden. Whether or not you have a green thumb, this unique stuffing with a toasted tarragon garnish will win rave reviews.

2 sticks (1 cup) butter

3 medium carrots, peeled

2 large leeks, rinsed, trimmed to white parts only

2 ears corn, husks removed

1 pound butternut squash, peeled, seeded, cut into 1-inch cubes (about 2½ cups)

1 (12-ounce) package cornbread stuffing mix

1 pound pork sausage

1 cup chicken broth

½ teaspoon salt

¼ teaspoon black pepper

3 tablespoons coarsely chopped, fresh tarragon leaves

MAKES ABOUT 8 CUPS

Preheat oven to 450F (205C). Melt ½ cup of the butter in a small bowl in the microwave. Place carrots, leeks, corn, and squash in 13 × 9-inch baking pan. Pour melted butter over vegetables and turn to coat. Bake for 30 minutes, or until vegetables are tender. Let stand until cool to touch.

Place stuffing mix in a large bowl. Dice carrots and leeks and mix into stuffing. Scrape corn kernels from cob and add to stuffing. Divide squash into 2 batches. Dice one batch of squash and stir into stuffing until combined. Add remaining squash to food processor and process until pureed. Stir into stuffing until incorporated.

Remove sausage from casing and crumble into a large skillet. Cook, stirring occasionally, over medium-high heat until browned. Add to stuffing and mix well.

Melt remaining ½ cup butter and stir into stuffing with chicken broth until thoroughly moistened. Season with salt and pepper.

Reduce oven temperature to 350F (175C). Place mixture in a large casserole and bake for 15 to 20 minutes, or until top is crusty. (Or stuff mixture into body cavity and neck of turkey. Remove stuffing from cooked turkey before carving.)

Place tarragon on a baking sheet and cook for 5 minutes, or until toasted. Set aside.

Spoon stuffing into a serving dish and garnish with toasted tarragon. Serve warm. (Store covered in the refrigerator for up to 3 days.)

NOTE Stuffing may be made 1 day in advance if stored in an airtight container in the refrigerator. Bake as directed above or stuff the turkey just before cooking.

Molasses Sweet Potato Whip

When hosting many guests for Thanksgiving dinner, one may have to be inventive with mixing bowls and big containers to prepare all the side dishes. A stockpot, without a nonstick coating, is a good solution for this recipe because it will hold the large amount of potatoes that need to be whipped.

6 pounds sweet potatoes, washed, peeled, cut into 1-inch chunks

3 tablespoons molasses

3/4 cup heavy cream

1 teaspoon ground ginger

MAKES 12 SERVINGS

Place sweet potatoes in a large stockpot and cover with water. Bring to a boil over medium-high heat and cook until tender, about 15 minutes. Drain off the water and transfer to a large bowl or place the sweet potatoes back in stockpot.

Mash sweet potatoes until smooth. Add molasses, cream, and ginger, and whip until blended and fluffy. Spoon into a serving dish and serve warm. (Store covered in the refrigerator for up to 1 day; reheat before serving.)

Warm Cranberry Compote with Walnut Streusel Topping

As an alternative to opening a can, perk up your traditional cranberry dish with this easy compote.

2 pounds (about 7 cups) fresh cranberries, rinsed

1 1/3 cups water

2/3 cup sugar

2 tablespoons fresh lemon juice

1/3 cup unsalted butter, softened

1/2 cup packed light brown sugar

1/2 cup all-purpose flour

1/2 cup ground walnuts

MAKES ABOUT 5 CUPS

Place cranberries, water, sugar, and lemon juice in a large saucepan. Cook over medium heat, stirring occasionally, until cranberries are just tender and mixture thickens, about 15 minutes. Remove from heat. Transfer to a large casserole dish.

Preheat oven to 350F (175C). Mix together butter, brown sugar, flour, and walnuts until just combined and crumbly. Crumble brown sugar mixture over cranberries. Bake for 20 minutes until top is golden brown. Cool to room temperature.

Serve in casserole. (Store in an airtight container in the refrigerator for up to 3 days.)

Pecan–Pumpkin Pie

A remarkable blend of two favorites, pecan pie and pumpkin pie seem to be a match made in heaven! Make 2 pies for 12 servings.

Tart crust (page 45) or purchased unbaked pie crust

3 eggs

1 cup packed light brown sugar

1/2 cup canned pumpkin puree

1/2 cup corn syrup

2 tablespoons unsalted butter, melted

1 teaspoon vanilla extract

1 1/3 cups coarsely chopped pecans

Sweetened whipped cream

12 pecan halves for topping

MAKES 6 TO 8 SERVINGS

Prepare crust dough and chill.

Preheat oven to 425F (220C). Roll out chilled dough to a 10-inch circle about 1/4 inch thick on a heavily floured surface. Transfer dough circle to a 9-inch pie pan. Trim and crimp the edges of the dough. Line crust with foil. Place pie weights or dry beans over surface of crust to weigh it down during cooking. Bake crust for 8 minutes. Remove crust from oven and reduce oven temperature to 350F (175C). Remove weights and foil from crust.

Beat eggs, sugar, and pumpkin in a medium bowl until creamy. Beat in corn syrup, butter, and vanilla until smooth. Stir in chopped pecans until distributed throughout mixture. Pour pumpkin mixture into baked crust.

Cover edges of exposed crust with foil to avoid burning. Bake for 50 minutes and remove foil. Bake for 10 minutes more, or until a knife inserted off center comes out clean. Remove from oven and cool to room temperature.

Place dollops of sweetened whipped cream on pie and top each dollop with a pecan half. Cut into wedges and serve. (Store without whipped cream for up to 3 days, covered, in the refrigerator.)

Rustic Autumn Centerpiece in a Wooden Fruit Box

FROM CRAFT STORE: 1 (6.7-liter) bag green sphagnum moss; 1 (12 × 8-inch) wooden crate or box, 5 inches high; plastic wrap; 2 bricks green floral Oasis; 20 wheat stems; 12 strings raffia; 5 assorted size lotus pods; 4 pheasant feathers; 14 (6-inch) green wooden flower sticks with pointed ends; 10 plastic assorted gourds and miniature pumpkins (optional: use real gourds); 6 autumn leaves

FROM FLORIST: 15 yellow carnations; 20 yellow chrysanthemums; 10 yellow Solidaster sprays

Soak moss in water to rid it of dust and revive green color. Wring moss thoroughly dry with hands. Line bottom of wooden crate with plastic wrap. Immerse green floral Oasis bricks in water until soaked. Place Oasis inside middle of wooden box and cover top of Oasis with moss. Loosely fill in around sides of Oasis with moss.

Gather wheat stems in a bunch and wrap 4 raffia strings up stems to bind; tie off with bow. Insert gathered wheat stems into Oasis just left of center of wooden box. Insert 3 lotus pods into Oasis just right of center of wooden box. Insert pheasant feathers in a group behind wheat stems and close to back left corner of box. Trim carnation and chrysanthemum stems to 6-inch, 8-inch, and 10-inch lengths. Build arrangement starting from center. Insert taller stems into center around wheat and lotus pods and shorter stems toward edge of box. Trim Solidaster sprays to 6-inch lengths and fill in around arrangement. Fill in arrangement with remaining lotus pods and autumn leaves.

Insert pointed end of green wooden sticks into bottom of plastic or real gourds and insert around outer perimeter of arrangement. Loop 2 raffia strings together and tie in a big bow on the tip of a green flower stick. Repeat with remaining picks and raffia. Insert picks with raffia bows into arrangement to finish.

*Opposite page:
A rustic autumn centerpiece sets the
tone for Thanksgiving dinner.*

Vegetable Seed Packet and Corn Husk Favors on Napkins

For each place setting, buy the following:

FROM GROCERY OR CRAFT STORE: 1 dried cornhusk; 1 clothespin, preferably old-fashioned type (materials are available in packs of several items)

FROM NURSERY: 1 vegetable seed packet (seeds same as vegetable on chair back)

Soak dried corn husks for 5 minutes in hot water to soften. Pat husks dry. Slide a husk into clothespin until pin is at husk's midpoint. Tie husk into a knot that rests in front of clothespin. Attach a vegetable seed packet with a colorful label to each person's napkin using husk clothespin.

Harvest Wheat and Vegetable Chair Decor

For each chair, buy the following:

FROM CRAFT STORE: 2 yards 1-inch-wide cloth ribbon; 20 wheat stems, 1 yard green floral wire; assorted dried fall flowers (optional)

FROM GROCERY STORE: a sturdy vegetable, such as carrots or beets that matches the seed packet at the place setting

Divide wheat stems into 2 bunches each with 10 wheat stems each. Crisscross bunches at the stems midpoint and wrap 1-foot piece green floral wire around stems at midpoint to secure. Wrap ribbon twice around stems, covering wire and tie a knot in front; Long ribbon ends will be used later to secure wheat to chair. Using a skewer, poke a hole through the vegetable, from one side through to the other, toward the top. Insert a 1½-foot piece floral wire through hole to midpoint of wire and twist wire at vegetable back. For carrots with green leafy stems or corn with husks attach, wrap wire around stems or husks where they meet vegetable and twist-tie. Insert remainder of wire stems behind ribbon knot and around wheat stems. Secure vegetable to wheat by twisting wire ends at wheat back; clip excess wire. Place wheat with attached vegetable vertically in middle of chair back so wheat extends just above top of chair. Wrap ribbon around chair back, and then bring around in front of vegetable. Knot ribbon to secure wheat to chair and finish with a bow, making sure all wire is masked. Insert dried harvest flower stems behind ribbon in front of wheat for more color if desired.

Opposite page:
Even the chairs and napkins are decorated with corn husks, vegetables, and seed packets to complete the holiday theme.

An Art Deco Christmas

December 25, 1927

The Story of Christmas

A time to lift voices on high in celebration, this spiritual holiday has origins prior to the Christian savior's nativity. Ancient Romans celebrated Saturnalia, named after Saturn, god of agriculture, by feasting for days in late December. Another fete, held on December 25, honored the birth of the powerful sun god Mithra, an infant deity born of a rock. In Scandinavia, a period of revelry known as Yule had a similar purpose as the others, a way of enduring a harsh winter and looking forward to a bountiful spring.

By the fourth century, the Church decided to set aside a day in honor of Christ's birth. Even though there is no mention of the actual birthday in the Bible, church officials selected a date of January 6 to coincide with the winter celebrations. Some accounts say that in A.D. 354, Bishop Liberus of Rome set the date of December 25 as Christ's Mass. The more popular belief is that Pope Julius I designated December 25 as the Feast of the Nativity. The holiday was widely celebrated from Egypt to England by

In 1610, tinsel, made of real silver, is invented in Germany.

DECEMBER
Read a New Book Month

National Pie Day
(December 1)

National Whiners' Day
(December 26)

the end of the sixth century. Today, Greek and Russian Orthodox churches still observe Christmas on January 6. The day is also referred to as Epiphany and Three Kings Day, commemorating the time when the three wise men found Jesus in the manger.

The earliest English recordings of Christmas Day as December 25 did not appear until 1043. Although the holiday now had a Christian connection, many still spent the day as they did during the winter festivals of ancient Rome, with drunken abandon and lascivious behavior. In the early seventeenth century, the Puritans, led by Oliver Cromwell, felt that the disorderly conduct of those celebrating was unsuitable for this occasion and they were able to cancel Christmas. Fortunately, Charles II was restored to the throne, and brought back the holiday. When Christmas finally arrived in America, the day was still wrought with conflict. The Puritans, trying to abolish the day, outlawed it in Boston from about 1659 to 1681, and those caught observing Christmas were fined. Happily, as America became more independent, Christmas was no longer a crime but a celebratory time!

Christmas was declared a national holiday on June 26, 1870. Most Christians come home from wherever they are, embracing Christmas as a cherished and sacred time spent with family and friends.

Festive Traditions and Folklore

A magical time of folklore and religious significance, this holiday warms one's heart and soul. You may wonder why we've chosen the Art Deco era for our celebration. This was the time when our image of Santa Claus with his rosy cheeks and red fur suit was firmly planted in our minds.

Many Christmas customs and traditions revolve around the act of giving and celebrating life. Families remember their ancestors as they place heirloom ornaments on the Christmas tree. Daughters bake their mothers' fruitcake recipe as handed down from grandma. Fathers and sons arrange lights on the house and reindeer on the roof. And many read " 'Twas the Night Before Christmas" to young ones too excited to sleep, with visions of Santa sliding down the chimney laden with toys. Although the rituals of this holiday are carried on from one generation to the next, many add new traditions into their celebration as a way of sparking the true meaning of Christmas to their children.

Santa Claus

Santa Claus was actually a real man named Saint Nicholas. Born in what we now call Turkey in the fourth century, this popular bishop was legendary for his love of children and his generosity.

One story of Saint Nick tells how he disguised himself and begged for money. He then gave the collection to the needy. Another popular tale tells how Saint Nicholas's charity helped three sisters marry, as their father was a poor man with no dowry to offer suitors. When the first daughter was to be wed, Saint Nicholas anonymously dropped a bag of gold down the chimney. When helping the other two daughters in the same secretive way, he was caught in the act and word of his philanthropy soon spread around the land.

Saint Nicholas first found his way into the American culture near the end of the eighteenth century. Back then our image of Santa was a man dressed in white with long robes and a pontifflike hat. In 1809, Washington Irving wrote *A History of New York,* and in a revised version in 1812 he poked fun at the Dutch holiday figure Sinter Klaas. Clement Moore, whose ownership has been questioned recently of the 1822 poem entitled "An Account of a Visit from Saint Nicholas" described Santa as "a right jolly old elf" flying though the air with a miniature sleigh and eight tiny reindeer. But in 1881, political cartoonist Thomas Nast illustrated Santa in *Harper's Weekly* as a plump, cheerful man with a white beard, holding a sack full of toys for children. Nast, drawing on folklore, gave Santa his red suit trimmed with white fur, North Pole home, elves in a workshop, and Mrs. Claus.

It was *The New York Times* that brought all the myths and legends together in 1927, describing the image and story of the magical Santa we know today. Coca-Cola's holiday advertising brought him to the rest of the country. In 1931, Haddon Sundblom, an illustrator for Coca-Cola, created clever advertisements each Christmas of Santa Claus at work. Children across the world know him by many names but all know Saint Nick as the one who brings toys to all the good little girls and boys on Christmas Day.

"White Christmas," sung by Bing Crosby, is released in 1942. This is the best-selling Christmas song of all time, with one hundred million copies sold.

Christmas Trees

The Christmas tree is a prominent symbol of this holiday all over the world. It is widely thought that Germans started the tradition of an indoor Christmas tree in the sixteenth century, and Protestant reformer Martin Luther was the first to make it shine. On his way home one winter evening Luther was awestruck by the twinkling stars and, wanting to recapture their brilliance, placed lit candles on his tree. In England in 1841, a sketch of the royal family around a holiday tree was depicted in the *Illustrated London News,* and the custom caught on in Britain. History tells us that the Pennsylvania Germans had community trees in America as early as 1747. But in 1848, a newspaper printed a picture of a Christmas tree, which popularized the tradition in the United States.

By the 1890s, Christmas ornaments had made their way to the United States from Germany and other parts of Europe, but most Americans decorated their trees with homemade trinkets, fruits, nuts, sweets, and candles. Fortunately, the invention of electricity enabled us to replace the unsafe practice of candles on the tree with strings of lights.

Christmas trees illuminate every town square across the country during the Yuletide season, reminding us all to be a little nicer to one another. Since 1933, the Christmas tree at Rockefeller Center has been a national treasure, but the true beauty of this symbol of life, love, and happiness can be felt gazing at its magnificent image in the window of a holiday home.

The Star Topping the Tree

The crowning glory of the tree, the star's "light" is a metaphor for the season. The Christmas holiday is an enlightened time for all to be aware of kindness, love, and generosity. Many Christians believe the star on top of the Christmas tree represents the star that lit up the sky leading the three wise men to Jesus in the manger.

Stocking Hanging on the Fireplace

As legend has it, when Saint Nicholas dropped a bag of gold down the chimney as dowry for a poor man's betrothed daughter, it fell into a stocking that was hung to dry on the fireplace. We hang Christmas stockings today hoping Santa will drop gifts into them.

Gift Giving and Mall Santas

Stores began to publicize Christmas shopping in 1820, and by mid-century newspapers had holiday sections advertising a real live Santa in the stores for children to visit. This snowballed into the gift-giving bonanza we know today, as many parents couldn't resist buying more trinkets for their darlings, especially after they had personally told Santa what they wished for.

Sending Christmas Cards

Each year Christmas cheer is sent to friends and family by the millions through the U.S. Postal Service. It all began in the 1840s when an English artist, John Calcott Horsley, began to make small cards featuring Christmas scenes and a holiday verse. A Massachusetts printer, Louis Prang, printed the first Christmas card in America in 1875. He increased the popularity of Christmas cards by running contests for the best card design. In Albany, New York, R. H. Pease also manufactured Christmas cards.

Kissing Under The Mistletoe

The touted myths of mistletoe range from powers of fertility to a secret remedy for disease, although it should be noted that the plant is poisonous. For centuries people have kissed under the holiday sprig in hopes of falling in love, reconciling differences, and wishing one well. Proper mistletoe protocol dictates that the man removes a berry when he kisses a woman. When all the berries are gone, the kissing is done.

Christmas Carols

Caroling is believed to have started in England around the Middle Ages. As was the custom on many holidays, those hoping for a donation of

America's mail volume rises 13 percent for the holiday season 2000. Part of that volume includes some of the 2.6 billion Christmas cards that are sent.

In 2001, more than 1.76 billion candy canes will be made for the Christmas season, resulting in many red tongues.

food or money sang songs as they traveled from house to house. Today we carol with our neighbors and at holiday parties, because it always fills us with the Christmas spirit.

Rudolph the Red-Nosed Reindeer

We all delight in the tale of the underdog reindeer turned hero who saved Christmas by lighting Santa's way through a foggy night.

In 1939, Montgomery Ward's department store publicized a Christmas poem written by employee Robert L. May to boost holiday sales. The story of the red-nosed marvel became a seasonal favorite when Gene Autry sang the tale of Rudolph in 1949 and Burl Ives narrated the clay character television version in 1964.

The Yule Log

The Norse are believed by some to have started the tradition of the Yule log. During the ancient midwinter festival of Yule, the people would light a log in their hearths and celebrate until the log burned out. Yule is derived from the Norse word *hweol*, meaning "wheel," as they believed the sun to be a wheel of fire.

Fruitcake and Eggnog!

We have to mention the poor, misunderstood fruitcake! Many give a fruitcake loaf to friends and family as a symbol of the sweetness of the season. Packed with red and green cherries, nuts, pineapples, and anything candied, this little cake becomes so heavy that some jokingly refer to it as an edible paperweight. Nog is an offshoot of grog, which refers to a rum drink. Records show that eggnog has been a part of the Christmas celebration since it was first drunk in the Jamestown settlement in 1607.

Christmas Dinner for Six

An artistic menu full of fabulous food will be both a visual and edible delight at your 1920s Art Deco Christmas table. Many home chefs use this auspicious occasion to create new dishes to serve along with their family recipes. This menu offers the opportunity to flaunt your culinary skills by blending vintage holiday fare with inventive presentation techniques.

A time when people swallowed goldfish and grown men wore raccoon coats, anything went in the twenties. With Prohibition in effect, those looking for a little spirit and a lot of fun flocked to speakeasies and sipped bathtub gin. In stark contrast to the devil-may-care attitude that epitomized the Roaring Twenties, Emily Post penned *Etiquette in Society, in Business, in Politics and at Home* in 1922. Indeed this decade was a roller coaster of ways and means that came to a crashing halt on October 29, 1929.

Along with a Merry Christmas we hope that you'll have an adventure in gastronomy reflective of the era's escapades.

Bow-Tied Presents of Filet Mignon with Madeira Sauce

Champagne Honey Carrots

Mushroom and Gruyère Timbales

Tossed green salad

Peppermint Chocolate Cake with White Chocolate Ganache Frosting

Merlot and Sparkling Punch

Bow-Tied Presents of Filet Mignon with Madeira Sauce

An obvious takeoff on beef Wellington, this artfully wrapped dish tastes as good as it looks.

2 tablespoons butter, plus extra for attaching bows

1 tablespoon Madeira wine

6 (8-ounce) filet mignon steaks, about 1½ inches thick

1 teaspoon salt

½ teaspoon black pepper

1 (17.3-ounce) package frozen puff pastry, thawed

1 egg yolk, lightly beaten

MADEIRA SAUCE

1½ cups beef broth (made from bouillon cubes)

1½ cups Madeira wine

3 medium shallots, cut into slivers

4 tablespoons butter

MAKES 6 SERVINGS

To prepare filets: Preheat oven to 425F (220C). Melt the 2 tablespoons butter with Madeira in small bowl in microwave. Brush melted butter mixture over filets and rub with salt and pepper. Insert a meat thermometer into a filet. Place in a 13 × 9-inch glass baking dish and bake 15 to 20 minutes, or until browned, and meat thermometer registers 140F (60C) for rare meat and 170F (75C) for well-done meat (see Note below). Cool filets and cover with plastic wrap. Chill until cold, at least 1 hour.

When ready to serve, preheat oven to 425F (220C). Spray a clean 13 × 9-inch baking pan with nonstick cooking spray.

Cut 2 puff pastry sheets crosswise into 1-inch-wide strips. Lay a strip of puff pastry across filet with strip ends extending down filet sides. Tuck strip ends under filet. Lay another strip over filet perpendicular to first strip and down sides; tuck ends under filet. Place filets in prepared baking dish and brush pastry very lightly with beaten egg yolk. Insert a meat thermometer in one filet.

Spray a baking sheet with nonstick cooking spray. To make puff pastry bows, gently stretch a puff pastry strip to 20 inches long. Form a bow on prepared sheet. Make bow loops large, as pastry will puff making loopholes much smaller. Make 6 bows and brush pastry very lightly with beaten egg yolk.

Place the pan with filets on upper rack in oven and place baking sheet with bows on lower rack. Bake for 10 to 12 minutes, or until pastry bows are puffed and golden brown. Remove bows from oven. Bake filets for an additional 8 to 10 minutes, or until meat thermometer registers desired doneness. Pastry on filets will not puff as much as bows but should be a golden brown when done.

Meanwhile, to make Madeira Sauce: Add beef broth, Madeira, and shallots to a large skillet and cook over high heat until mixture boils and reduces to 1¼ cups, 20 to 25 minutes. Remove from heat and swirl in butter, 1 tablespoon at a time, until combined.

Using a spatula, remove filets from baking dish, being careful to keep wrapped puff pastry strips intact. Remove pastry bows in same fashion. Place a tiny dab of butter on top of pastry on filets and place bow on butter.

Arrange filets on a serving platter or individual plates. Spoon 2 to 3 tablespoons sauce around each filet (spooning sauce over filets will make puff pastry soggy). Serve hot.

NOTE Do not overcook the filets as they will be cooked again with puff pastry wrapping. Cook filets the first time to an internal temperature just under your desired doneness. When the filets are cooked a second time they will be put in the oven cold. They will reheat and cook slightly to an internal temperature of about 10 degrees higher than the first thermometer reading.

Champagne Honey Carrots

Placed in a menu abundant with cream, these champagne-laced carrots are nice and light.

1 tablespoon olive oil

3 tablespoons butter

1 shallot, minced

2 pounds baby carrots

1 cup dry Champagne

2 tablespoons honey

1 sprig fresh thyme

⅛ teaspoon salt

⅛ teaspoon white pepper

MAKES 8 SERVINGS

Heat oil and butter in a large skillet over medium-high heat. Add shallot and carrots and cook, stirring occasionally, until carrots are just tender, 15 to 20 minutes. Stir in Champagne, honey, and thyme and cook, stirring occasionally, until liquid reduces to one fourth, 3 to 5 minutes. Remove from heat and discard thyme. Stir in salt and pepper.

Transfer to a serving bowl. Serve warm. (Store covered in plastic wrap for up to 2 days in the refrigerator; reheat before serving.)

Mushroom and Gruyère Timbales

This cup-shaped custard with mushrooms and cheese is a beautiful side dish for elegant meals.

2 tablespoons butter

2 tablespoon olive oil

1 large brown onion, minced

1 pound button mushrooms, finely minced

1¼ cups freshly grated Gruyère cheese

½ teaspoon salt

¼ teaspoon black pepper

¾ cup heavy cream

6 eggs

3 tablespoons minced red bell pepper

3 tablespoons minced green bell pepper

MAKES ABOUT 12 TIMBALES

Heat butter and oil in a large skillet over medium-high heat. Add onion and cook, stirring occasionally, until translucent, 3 to 5 minutes. Add mushrooms and cook, stirring occasionally, until mushrooms are tender and liquid evaporates, about 10 minutes. Transfer mushrooms to a large bowl. Stir in cheese, salt, and black pepper until combined.

Preheat oven to 325F (165C). Line 12 cups of a muffin pan with foil cups. Spray cups with nonstick cooking spray. Beat cream and eggs in a large bowl until just blended. Pour egg mixture into mushroom mixture and stir until combined.

Pour mixture into prepared foil cups. Fill a large baking pan halfway with hot water. Set muffin pan inside pan of water and place on lower rack of oven. Bake 35 to 40 minutes, or until a knife inserted off center of a timbale comes out clean. Carefully remove from oven to avoid spilling hot water. Remove muffin pan from water. Cool for 10 minutes.

Remove timbales from muffin pan and gently peel away foil cups. Place upside down on a serving platter or individual plates and garnish with red and green peppers. Serve immediately. (Store covered in the refrigerator for up to 2 days; reheat in oven before serving.)

Peppermint Chocolate Cake with White Chocolate Ganache Frosting

Candy canes and chocolate, a popular combination in many a child's dream, are outstanding in this luscious Christmas dessert.

CHOCOLATE CAKE

2 cups sugar

2 cups all-purpose flour

1/2 cup unsweetened cocoa powder

1 1/2 teaspoons baking powder

1 teaspoon baking soda

1/8 teaspoon salt

3 eggs

3/4 cup unsalted butter, melted and cooled

2 teaspoons peppermint extract

1 cup milk

1/2 cup warm water

10 large candy canes

CHOCOLATE MOUSSE FILLING

2 recipes Chocolate Espresso Mousse (page 9)

WHITE CHOCOLATE GANACHE FROSTING

1 1/3 cups heavy cream

9 ounces good-quality white chocolate, chopped (about 1 1/3 cups)

MAKES ABOUT 12 SERVINGS

To make cake: Preheat oven to 350F (175C). Cut waxed paper rounds to fit the bottom of 2 (8-inch) round cake pans. Butter pans and place waxed paper rounds in bottoms. Butter waxed paper.

Sift together sugar, flour, cocoa, baking powder, baking soda, and salt into a large bowl. Add eggs, butter, peppermint extract, and milk, and beat for 2 minutes. Add water and beat until blended. Divide batter evenly between prepared pans. Place pans on center rack in oven.

Bake 30 to 40 minutes, or until a wooden pick inserted in cake center comes out clean. Cool in pans on wire racks for 10 minutes. Gently run knife around cake edges to loosen cakes from pans and invert onto wire racks. Peel waxed paper away from cake bottoms and place right side up on wire racks. Cool completely.

To make filling: Follow directions for Chocolate Espresso Mousse on page 9, doubling the recipe and omitting the espresso powder and Kahlúa. Prepare mousse in a large bowl and refrigerate covered with plastic wrap until mousse becomes slightly firm, about 2 hours.

To fill: Place a cake round on a serving plate. Spread mousse filling in a thick, even layer over top. (You may not need to use all of the mousse.) Place the other cake round on top of filling. Wrap plastic wrap around sides of cake to keep mousse from seeping out between layers. Refrigerate until frosting is ready.

To make frosting: Heat cream in a small saucepan over medium-low heat until just about to boil. Place white chocolate in a heatproof bowl. Pour hot cream over chocolate and stir until smooth. Cool for 15 minutes. Cover and refrigerate until mixture thickens slightly and is cold, at least 3 hours.

Beat chilled frosting until mixture thickens into a stiff, whipped cream consistency, 3 to 5 minutes. Remove plastic wrap from sides of cake. Spread frosting over cake, icing top and sides completely. Break crooked tops off whole candy canes and set aside. Break remaining candy-cane stems into large pieces and arrange on top and around base of cake. Insert candy-cane tops into top of cake. Refrigerate cake until ready to serve.

Place whole cake on table and cut into wedges to serve. (Store covered in plastic wrap in the refrigerator for up to 1 week.)

VARIATION To match the photo of this cake decorate the sides of the cake with different colored, seasonal candies.

Calla Lily and Dangling Crystal Chandelier Wreath

FROM FLORIST: 1 (18-inch-diameter) mâché-backed wreath containing green floral Oasis; 1 large-leaf ivy plant with 4-foot-long vines; 20 magnolia leaves; 15 calla lilies; 15 tree fern sprays

FROM CRAFT STORE: 2 (6.7-liter) bags green sphagnum moss; Tack 2000 wet floral spray adhesive; 8 dried pomegranates; 8 seasonal plastic berry sprays on a pick; silver metallic spray paint; 30-foot (2-inch-wide) sturdy, white cloth ribbon; 8 green wooden flower picks; 15 oversized, pear-shaped, clear, acrylic, faceted rhinestones with drilled hole for jewelry loop; 5 feet 22-gauge metal wire

This wreath is hung from the ceiling as a chandelier; remember as you arrange the flowers and greenery that the bottom and sides are the most visible. You may wish to replace a lamp hanging over the center of your dining-room table with this wreath and hang the wreath from an existing ceiling hook. MAKE SURE YOUR CEILING HOOK HAS BEEN PROPERLY INSTALLED AND IS SCREWED INTO AN INTERNAL CEILING RAFTER OR WOOD STUD. Don't guess at this, ask a professional to install a hook properly to hold the weight of this wreath. If there is any doubt that the hook will not hold the wreath, place the wreath directly on the table as a centerpiece. Do not hang this wreath from an expensive crystal chandelier or lamp. If you intend to hang the wreath on a door in a traditional manner, dangle the rhinestones from the wreath's front.

Work on a surface covered with plastic. The day before you make this craft, soak moss in water to rid moss of dust and revive green color. Wring moss thoroughly dry with hands. Pour water over Oasis in wreath until Oasis is soaked. Spray Tack 2000 over entire surface including mâché bottom of wreath. Adhere moss to wreath to cover completely. Spray dried pomegranates and seasonal berry picks with sliver spray paint. Allow paint to dry completely.

Insert branch end of 4-foot ivy vine into Oasis and wrap vine around wreath leaving 2 inches between vine winds. Cut 4 (6-foot-long) pieces of ribbon. Loop each ribbon through wreath center, under, and around outside of wreath. Place 4 ribbons at equal points around wreath; it will hang from ceiling supported by looped ribbon. Even up ribbon ends so wreath will hang level and tightly knot ends together. With additional ribbon tie a big bow just below knot.

Insert stems of magnolia leaves into Oasis around wreath in between 4 ribbon points. Cut calla lily stems to 5-inch lengths and insert stems into Oasis around wreath in same fashion. Insert pointed end of green wooden flower picks into silver pomegranates. Insert picks with silver pomegranates and berries around wreath to decorate. Cut tree fern sprays to 6-inch lengths and fill in wreath with greenery.

A calla lily and crystal wreath hangs above this Christmas table.

Using wire cutters, cut 22-gauge wire into 15 (4-inch) lengths and feed wire through holes in rhinestones. Wrap rhinestone wire around ivy vine at different points around wreath bottom and sides so stones will dangle from hung wreath; twist wire to tie and clip excess. Hang wreath from secure ceiling hook under ribbon knot.

Christmas Tree Spiral Around a Napkin with Jeweled Place-Card Clip Topper

For each spiral, buy the following:

FROM CRAFT STORE: 60 black and 60 clear iridescent, bi-cone (5mm), faceted, plastic, or acrylic beads; 2 feet 22-gauge metal wire

FROM HOME OR FLEA MARKET: Christmas-themed, costume jewelry, clip-on earrings

FROM STATIONERY STORE: Place cards

Thread wire through first bead and bend ½ inch of wire end around bead to secure. Thread beads on wire, repeating a pattern of 10 blacks beads and 10 clear beads. Wrap wire end around last bead to secure. Fold cloth napkin on diagonal, making a triangle. Fold triangle in half and then fold in half again, making a 6-inch-high triangle with 12-inch-long side. Roll corners of each long side into back center of napkin, forming a pointed bishop's-hat shape. Insert straight pin into rolls to temporarily keep napkin shape. Starting at back of napkin, spiral beaded wire up around napkin to top. Stand upright at place setting and remove straight pin. Clip on costume jewelry earring at wire top and napkin point to resemble star topping Christmas tree. Slide guest's place card under jeweled clip in front.

Costume-Jewelry Pin Fasteners for Organza Chair Overlays

For each chair, buy the following:

FROM FABRIC STORE: 3 yards (60-inch-wide) crystal organza

FROM HOME OR FLEA MARKET: Christmas-themed, costume-jewelry pin.

Drape fabric over chair so length of fabric covers chair from front to back. Allow enough slack in fabric to cover chair seat comfortably. Loosely pull back the fabric that is hanging from either side of chair so both sides of fabric meet behind chair. Pin fabric together at center back of chair with costume-jewelry pin.

Opposite page:
Christmas tree spirals guide guests
to their places at the table.

A New Year's Eve
of High Expectations

The Story of
New Year's Eve

JANUARY

National Oatmeal Month

Procrastinators' New Year (January 15)

National Kazoo Day (January 28)

The joyous celebration of the New Year is probably the world's oldest. Many cultures have their own annual beginning, but we've chosen to explore the journey of time as expressed in the Gregorian calendar, which is the one used to mark each passing day in the United States.

Two thousand years ago and then some, it is believed that ancient Babylonians began their new year with the first new moon after the spring equinox. A logical time to celebrate, spring brings with it new growth and has always been symbolic of hope and the promise of things to come. The Babylonians feasted for eleven days, each day with its own festive theme.

Fast-forward to Julius Caesar, who, during a visit to Egypt around 150 B.C., found the calendar of his dreams. The Romans tried to follow the same cycle as the Egyptians, with the New Year beginning in spring. But scholars and emperors continued to finagle with the calendar until it fell out of sync with the sun. The Roman Senate, in an attempt to get everything back on track, named January 1 as the first day of the year, and eventually their calendar was called the Julian calendar.

Still the calendar was constantly being revised and manipulated by various people, until 1582, when Pope Gregory XIII established the Gregorian calendar. This calendar set the dates and offered a clear demarcation of the four seasons. The Gregorian calendar is what most of the Western world uses today.

We welcome January 1 with bells, noisemakers, and people shouting "Happy New Year." We kiss, toast, sing, and make a resolution to do better in the coming year.

Festive Traditions and Folklore

The stroke of midnight was never so sound as the one on December 31, 1999. Full of hope, reminiscences, and a little trepidation this monumental occasion was a once in a lifetime occurrence that moved us all. Another one thousand years, what a great reason to party, and the celebrations were tremendous, whether that meant sipping champagne in front of the Eiffel Tower or kissing your baby at midnight as he slept peacefully at home. This was a very personal event that people considered carefully before they decided how and where to celebrate.

Few New Year's traditions have changed over the years but one thing's for certain; confetti sales soar around the holiday. The ultimate time of jubilation and anticipation, we hope you find a way to make this New Year's celebration and the next 365 days a smashing success.

Auld Lang Syne

An old Scottish lyric written by Robert Burns in the eighteenth century, "Auld Lang Syne" is nostalgically sung at the stroke of midnight amid the clamor of noisemakers and kissing couples. The literal translation of the title is "old long ago," or simply "the good old days." First published in 1796 after Burn's death, this poetic song is sung in almost every English-speaking country in the world to welcome in the New Year. The funny thing is that although we sing it every year, many are unsure of the words.

Champagne Toast

Liveliness in a glass, a champagne toast at midnight is a long-standing tradition. Probably French in origin, something bubbly, be it champagne or sparkling water, is always a festive way to commemorate a special occasion.

Kissing Your Loved One at Midnight

It is customary to kiss the one you love or hope to love at midnight as if to say, "Congratulations to us for making it through another year!"

Noisemakers

Church bells ring and people make a lot of noise all around the world when the clock strikes midnight. This tradition is believed to derive from the ancient belief that if a person was loud and made enough of an uproar, he could drive evil spirits away.

New Year's Resolution

Whether it is a silent promise to oneself to stop telling white lies or a big declaration of an intent to lose weight, a New Year's resolution is a must. Many find it easier to make a fresh beginning as symbolized by January 1.

Baby New Year and Father Time

The tradition of a "Baby New Year" is said to have started in Greece around 600 B.C. In celebration of Dionysus, god of wine, a baby in a basket represented the annual rebirth of the god. Today, Baby New Year symbol-

Betsy Ross was born January 1, 1752. Ross was a well-known seamstress during the American Revolution and is believed to have stitched the first American flag.

On New Year's Day in 1863, President Abraham Lincoln issues the Emancipation Proclamation, which abolishes slavery in the United States.

izes the young year, and Father Time the year just passed. Fourteenth-century Germans are credited with the first visual use of the symbol—a New Year's banner with the image of a baby on it.

Times Square and The Big Ball

Since 1904, Times Square in New York City has been a hot spot for New Year's Eve celebrations. Originally the owners of the square held rooftop parties, and now the streets are flooded with people who brave the freezing cold just to watch the big ball drop. The first time the ball took the plunge was on New Year's Eve, 1907. Originally, the Times Square ball was made of iron and wood and decorated with one hundred (twenty-five-watt) lightbulbs. For New Year, 2001, half a million people gazed at the sphere made of Waterford crystal and lit by six-hundred bulbs as it dropped from the top of a skyscraper at midnight. Adored TV veteran Dick Clark first aired *New Year's Rocking Eve* in 1972, and has broadcast the show live from Times Square ever since.

The Tournament of Roses Parade

In 1886 members of the Valley Hunt Club decorated their carriages with flowers and paraded through Pasadena, California, celebrating the ripe orange crop. Today large, elaborate floats, covered with flowers, nuts, and anything natural, join in the pageantry of the Tournament of Roses parade. The Rose Bowl, a football game, has traditionally followed the parade since 1902 with a brief "time-out" when the sport was replaced with Roman chariot races in 1903. Thirteen years later, much to its fans' delight, football made a comeback!

The Mummers' Parade

A Philadelphia tradition with beginnings in the 1700s, the mummers' parade is based on European models, particularly those of the Swedes and English. The Swedish tradition of continuing Christmas celebrations into the New Year was combined with the English tradition of mummery. Initially marked by musket fire and a noisy parade, mummers went from house to house, dressed up or with blackened faces, shouting, shooting, and chanting in hopes of receiving spirits, money, and cakes. Today mummers still chant, dress in hilarious costumes, and are as loud as can be during this twelve-hour parade.

The Polar Bear Swim

In British Columbia, and other freezing parts of the world, people plunge into the ice-cold water and take the traditional polar bear swim on New Year's Day. Some say it's "just plain fun," whereas others look at the frigid frolic as a reminder that "it's great to be alive for another year!"

Lucky Food for a Lucky Year

In the United States, black-eyed peas, specifically in a dish called Hoppin' John, is a popular and lucky New Year's Day food. The peas are usually mixed with rice and hog jowls, a harbinger of wealth, as in the phrase "livin' high on the hog." Cabbage is also eaten on New Year's Day, as the green leaves are representative of paper currency and prosperity. Many share the belief that food shaped like a ring, such as doughnuts, completes the year and tops off the tummy.

New Year's Customs Around the World

Our friends around the world have wonderful traditions for welcoming the New Year.

In Rio de Janeiro, people go to the beaches to watch fireworks and take a midnight dip in the water; offering flowers and a wish to the goddess Lemanja. The English look to the "first-footer" or the first

On New Year's Day in 1892, Ellis Island is opened. Over twenty million immigrants will land on this island in New York Harbor to start a new life in America before it closes in 1954.

person to set foot into their house to tell them how next year's luck will be.

New Year's Day marks the Festival of Saint Basil in Greece; children leave their shoes out to be filled with gifts. Saint Basil's Bread is baked with small trinkets inside, bringing luck to those who find them.

Italians hang mistletoe over the front door to bring good luck. Women in Mexico wear red underwear if they wish to marry in the New Year, and pink is worn by pregnant women to bring luck to their babies. Those hoping to travel carry an empty suitcase around the block. Many people in Spain and Latin countries eat twelve grapes at midnight as a bell is rung twelve times. Each grape represents a month of the year. By eating them at midnight one hopes to have happiness and luck for the next twelve months.

New Year's Eve
Hors d'Oeuvres Party for Eighteen

An hors d'oeuvres party with an international flair best suits this technologically supreme decade as the advancements have made the world a smaller place. The nineties were a melting pot for cuisine. Not only did we all have permission from food gurus to experiment in the kitchen, we could obtain just about any product we desired with the point and click of a mouse. It's all about access. At the culinary forefront were food and "how-to" networks, which allowed viewers to watch an Italian chef at 3 P.M. and become a pasta pro by 6 P.M. . . . just in time for dinner!

As we sped toward the millennium, one thing was on everyone's mind. With what champagne will I raise my glass to ring in the New Year? Given the fear that kept some from going out to celebrate, it was comforting to have the heartfelt tradition of toasting loved ones at midnight. There's nothing like a little bubbly to put one in a festive mood.

Teriyaki Tuna Skewers

Polenta Griddle Cakes with Goat Cheese and Tomatillo Chutney

Tandoori Chicken-Filled Roti Rolls with Pachadi Dipping Sauce

Open-Face California Rolls on Edamame Rice Squares

Champagne or sparkling water

Teriyaki Tuna Skewers

Many prefer tuna seared or just barely cooked. If you intend to prepare these skewers on the rare side, tell the person from whom you are buying the fish that you want the highest quality or "sushi grade." If sushi grade is unavailable, prepare the fish well-done.

1 pound sushi-grade tuna steak fillets	2 tablespoons light brown sugar
6 tablespoons soy sauce	1 teaspoon minced fresh ginger
6 tablespoons sherry	3 tablespoons toasted sesame seeds
2 teaspoons fresh lemon juice	2 tablespoons minced chives

MAKES ABOUT 20 APPETIZERS

Slice tuna fillets crosswise to ⅛-inch thickness, making 3 X 1-inch strips.

Whisk together soy sauce, sherry, lemon juice, brown sugar, ginger, sesame seeds, and chives in a small bowl until combined. Arrange tuna strips in flat layer in a glass baking dish. Pour marinade over tuna. Cover and refrigerate for 30 minutes. Soak 20 bamboo skewers in water 30 minutes.

Preheat grill or broiler. Thread a bamboo skewer through each tuna strip 2 times so strip is secure.

NOTE Do not marinade fish or chicken in a marinade with citrus for long periods of time, as the citrus will break down the meat, resulting in a mealy texture.

Grill tuna skewers over medium-high heat on a grill or grill pan without sides so tuna may lie flat and cook evenly. Cook for 2 to 3 minutes, then turn skewers over. Cook until tuna loses its dark purple color, 2 to 3 minutes more.

Arrange on a serving tray and serve immediately.

Polenta Griddle Cakes with Goat Cheese and Tomatillo Chutney

An eclectic collection of flavor sensations, as corn cakes are topped with sweet tangy chutney and accented by goat cheese. These little tidbits will add a colorful flair to your hors d'oeuvres tray.

POLENTA GRIDDLE CAKES

2 cups chicken broth

1 cup cornmeal

1/4 teaspoon salt

Corn oil, for cooking

1/4 cup crumbled goat cheese

TOMATILLO CHUTNEY

6 tomatillos (3/4 pound), husks removed

1 clove garlic, minced

1 teaspoon minced jalapeño chile pepper

1/2 cup chopped cilantro leaves

1/2 cup diced red onion

1/4 cup packed light brown sugar

1/3 cup white wine vinegar

1/4 cup golden raisins

1/8 teaspoon salt

MAKES ABOUT 24 APPETIZERS

Bring broth to a boil in a medium saucepan over medium heat. Slowly sprinkle cornmeal into broth while quickly whisking mixture. Continue whisking for 3 minutes, smoothing out any lumps as mixture thickens. Replace whisk with a wooden spoon and cook, stirring constantly, until mixture thickens, about 1 minute. Spoon should stand in mixture and polenta will come away from sides of pan. Remove from heat and stir in salt. Transfer to a bowl and let stand until cool to touch.

Form 1/4-inch-thick, silver-dollar-size patties using 2 teaspoons of mixture for each. Heat 1 teaspoon oil in a large skillet over medium-high heat. Add as many patties as skillet will hold and cook until underside is lightly browned, 2 to 3 minutes. Flip patties over with a spatula and cook until other side is lightly browned, 2 to 3 minutes. Remove from skillet and transfer to paper towels to drain off excess oil. Continue with remaining cakes, adding oil to the pan as needed. Cover cakes with plastic wrap while you prepare chutney.

To make chutney: Rinse tomatillos under warm water to remove stickiness and pat dry. Finely dice tomatillos and place in a medium saucepan. Add remaining ingredients and stir to combine. Cook, covered, over low heat for 30 minutes until ingredients are very tender. Makes about 1½ cups. (Store in an airtight container in the refrigerator for up to 1 week. Bring to room temperature or heat before serving.)

Spoon 1 teaspoon of warm chutney on cakes and top with 1/2 teaspoon crumbled goat cheese. Arrange on serving tray and serve warm. (Store extra cakes covered in plastic wrap in the refrigerator for 2 days.)

Tandoori Chicken-Filled Roti Rolls with Pachadi Dipping Sauce

We know what you're thinking. What in the world is "roti" and is "pachadi" a real word? Although tandori chicken is usually cooked in a special oven, we've made a mock version of the Indian classic using traditional spices. Roti is an Indian bread and the pachadi sauce is a mango-yogurt dip. This recipe may seem foreign, but it will soon be a familiar favorite.

4 boneless, skinless chicken breast halves, fat trimmed

3 cloves garlic, peeled

2-inch piece fresh ginger, peeled

½ teaspoon salt

1 teaspoon black pepper

1 teaspoon chili powder

1 teaspoon curry powder

½ teaspoon ground turmeric

½ teaspoon ground cumin

3 tablespoons plain yogurt

1 tablespoon fresh lemon juice

1 teaspoon sugar

1 drop orange food coloring

3 tablespoons olive oil

ROTI ROLLS
1½ cups whole-wheat flour

½ teaspoon salt, plus extra for sprinkling

⅛ teaspoon ground cumin

1 egg, lightly beaten

1 tablespoon butter, melted

1½ tablespoons olive oil

¼ cup warm water

Canola oil, for cooking

Pachadi Dipping Sauce (see recipe page 151)

MAKES ABOUT 30 ROLLS

Make diagonal incisions all over chicken and place in a baking dish. Using a mortar and pestle, grind garlic and ginger into a paste (see Note below).

Mix together the ginger-garlic paste, salt, pepper, chili powder, curry powder, turmeric, cumin, yogurt, lemon juice, sugar, and food coloring. Place chicken in a baking dish; smear mixture on chicken until completely coated. Cover with plastic wrap and refrigerate overnight.

Preheat oven to 375F (190C). Place chicken in a clean baking dish and brush with oil. Bake for 30 minutes, or until chicken is no longer pink in center. Remove from heat and let stand until cool to touch. Cut chicken crosswise into 1/16-inch-thick slices. Cut slices lengthwise into ¼-inch-wide strips.

To make roti rolls: Sift together flour, salt, and cumin into a large bowl. Make a well in the center of flour and add egg, butter, and olive oil. Using clean hands, knead mixture to combine. Add water, 1 tablespoon at a time, and knead until a stiff dough forms. Knead dough for about 5 minutes more. Cover dough with plastic wrap and allow to rest for 30 minutes at room temperature.

Roll out dough on a lightly floured surface to 1/8-inch thickness using a floured rolling pin. Using a sharp knife, cut dough into 3 × 1-inch rectangles.

Roll up 4 strips of chicken in a dough rectangle; Dough should be wrapped around middle of chicken strips with chicken sticking out of either end of roll similar to "pigs in a blanket." Press dough edge around middle to seal roll.

Heat 1/4 cup canola oil in a large skillet over medium-high heat. Add chicken rolls to skillet in batches and cook, turning rolls with tongs, until all sides of dough are lightly browned, a total of about 5 minutes. Remove from skillet and drain on paper towels. Repeat with remaining rolls, adding more oil if necessary.

NOTE If mortar and pestle are unavailable, mash garlic and ginger in a small bowl using the back of a spoon.

Cool 5 minutes and sprinkle lightly with salt. Arrange on a serving tray with a small bowl of pachadi dipping sauce on the side.

Pachadi Dipping Sauce

Use as a dipping sauce for tandoori chicken-filled roti rolls (page 150) or grilled chicken pieces.

3/4 cup finely diced mango	1 tablespoon shredded sweetened coconut
3/4 cup peeled, finely diced cucumber	1 teaspoon yellow curry powder
2 tablespoons minced red onion	2 cups plain yogurt
1/2 teaspoon minced green chile	1 1/2 teaspoons sugar

MAKES ABOUT 3 CUPS

Combine all ingredients in a small bowl and stir until combined. Serve as a dipping sauce.

Open-Face California Rolls on Edamame Rice Squares

Edamame, cooked green young soybeans, are a popular "freebie" in Japanese restaurants. A dish of beans in their pods is placed on the table as a complimentary starter just as bread and butter is offered in many restaurants.

SUSHI RICE

1½ cups short-grain rice

1½ cups water

⅓ cup seasoned rice wine vinegar

EDAMAME PUREE

½ pound green young soybeans in pods

1 tablespoon plus ⅛ teaspoon salt

1 teaspoon sesame oil

3 tablespoons water

FOR ASSEMBLY

1 cucumber, washed

1 ripe avocado

2 (6-ounce) cans crabmeat

1 (2-ounce) jar salmon roe or red lumpfish roe

1 bunch chives, rinsed, cut into 1-inch lengths

MAKES ABOUT 40 SQUARES

To make rice: Soak rice in a bowl of cold water. With clean hands, gently stir rice until water becomes cloudy. Strain rice in a sieve and set aside in sieve for 30 minutes to drain excess water.

Place rice in a medium pot and add the 1½ cups cold water. Cover and cook over medium-high heat until rice steams, 5 to 8 minutes. Turn heat to high and cook for 2 minutes more. Reduce heat to medium and cook for 5 minutes more, until you hear a crackling sound. Do not lift lid during cooking process. Turn off heat and allow rice to stand covered for 15 minutes.

Remove the lid and fluff the rice with a bamboo paddle or a wide wooden spoon. Cover and let stand another 15 minutes.

Spread rice along the bottom and up the sides of a large nonmetallic bowl or platter. Sprinkle vinegar over rice, quickly tossing rice with wooden paddle to incorporate vinegar. Fan rice with a paper fan or piece of cardboard for about 2 minutes. Cover bowl with a clean damp towel until rice cools to room temperature. Prepare sushi as soon as rice cools for maximum results. (Do not store rice in the refrigerator as chilled rice loses its stickiness.)

To make Edamame Puree: Fill a medium pot halfway with water and add 1 tablespoon salt. Bring to a boil over high heat. Add soybean pods and cook until tender, 5 minutes. Drain in a colander. Cool completely. Split pods and place beans in a bowl. Place beans, sesame oil, 3 tablespoons water, and ⅛ teaspoon salt into blender jar and puree until smooth.

To assemble: Slice cucumber crosswise into 1/16-inch-thick rounds. Quarter rounds into 4 wedges each. Cut avocado in half lengthwise and remove pit. Gently peel away skin and place avocado half, flat side down, on cutting board. Slice lengthwise into 1/16-inch-thick slices. Cut slices into wedges the same size as the cucumber wedges (see Note below). Drain any excess juice from crabmeat.

With moistened hands, form rice into flat squares using heaping 1 tablespoon rice per square. Gently smear 1/2 teaspoon bean puree in a thin layer over entire top of rice square. Place 3/4 teaspoon crab on top in center of square. Insert cucumber wedge and avocado wedge in middle of crab, pointed side up. Wedges should be artfully placed to resemble cat ears. Spoon a tiny amount of salmon roe in front of wedges. Insert a few chive lengths vertically into crab behind wedges. Chives should look like blades of grass coming up between wedge points.

NOTE Avocado pulp will brown very quickly when exposed to air. Cut avocado just before assembling hors d'oeuvres. Brush avocado with fresh lemon juice to keep from browning too quickly.

Arrange squares on a serving tray. Serve chilled.

New Year's Decor and Personal Touches

Champagne Glasses with Shiny Accents

FROM HARDWARE STORE: 1 (3-yard) roll 2-inch-wide foil tape (found near duct tape or in plumbing section).

These shapes are a wonderful accent on the outside of glassware and will help guests keep track of their glass. Cut shapes from foil tape such as diamonds, clubs, spades, hearts, moons, or stars. Try to avoid wrinkling tape and gently peel paper away from back of tape shape. Adhere shape to side of dry, inexpensive champagne glass. To remove, peel off foil tape and rub glue residue with nail-polish remover or similar substance.

Metallic mesh luminaries and accented champagne glasses add to the party atmosphere.

Metallic Mesh Luminaires

For each one, buy the following:

FROM 99-CENT STORE: 4 copper or silver mesh scrubbers (not Brillo pads or scouring pads)

FROM FLORIST OR CRAFT STORE: 8-inch-wide glass bubble bowl; 1 small floating tea candle, about the diameter of a silver dollar.

Fill a 6-inch-high, clear, sturdy drinking glass halfway with water. Place the tea candle in water and place drinking glass inside bubble bowl. (Do not place votive candles or tapers in bowl with mesh scrubbers as they will ignite.) For safety, candle must be floating in glass filled halfway with water, so flame is well contained. Drinking glass should be almost as high as bubble bowl. Using wire cutters, clip the little metal wire that holds the scrubber together and gently stretch out the mesh, which will result in a mesh tube. Put mesh tube into bubble bowl around the outside of drinking glass. Place 3 more mesh tubes into bowl and arrange mesh so it appears to fill bowl, but mesh must placed so it will not fall into drinking glass with lit candle. Light candle with long match and gaze at this stunningly simple luminaire.

New Year's Hors d'Oeuvres Trays

Found in the bath department of many large hardware stores, a 6-pack of mirror tiles costs around ten dollars. Tape edges with thin strip of foil tape for safety reasons or purchase mirror tiles with beveled edges, which cost a little more. These are great place mats, trays, or centerpiece liners.

Museum wax found in most hardware stores is the secret to keeping little arrangements and decor on trays intact, especially when trays are being passed. Place 1- to 2-tablespoon-size globs of museum wax where you want the arrangement. Insert flowers or decorative items into wax to completely cover wax and keep it from touching food on the tray. Although museum wax can be removed with silver polish, we don't recommend using the wax on your fine silver trays.

Orchid and Rock Salt Tray (photo on page 147): Rock salt, found at grocery stores, covers museum wax. Orchids are inserted in between salt into wax.

A mirror tile reflects orchids and Open-Face California Rolls on Edamame Rice Squares (page 152).

Festive trinkets adorn a tray holding Polenta Griddle Cakes with Goat Cheese and Tomatillo Chutney (page 149).

Peacock Feather and Flower Tray (147): Feathers are cut to desired length and inserted into wax in a fan design. Anthurium stems are trimmed and inserted with Galax leaves in front of feathers.

Metallic Fringed Horn and New Year's Trinket Trays (photo above): White whistle tip of party horns are inserted into wax with horns' metallic fringe end facing up so fringe flops over. Tiny plastic bottle poppers are placed around horn, stuck into wax.

Metric Conversion Charts

Comparison to Metric Measure

WHEN YOU KNOW	SYMBOL	MULTIPLY BY	TO FIND	SYMBOL
teaspoons	tsp.	5.0	milliliters	ml
tablespoons	tbsp.	15.0	milliliters	ml
fluid ounces	fl. oz.	30.0	milliliters	ml
cups	c	0.24	liters	l
pints	pt.	0.47	liters	l
quarts	qt.	0.95	liters	l
ounces	oz.	28.0	grams	g
pounds	lb.	0.45	kilograms	kg
Fahrenheit	F	$5/9$ (after subtracting 32)	Celsius	C

Fahrenheit to Celsius

F	C
200–205	95
220–225	105
245–250	120
275	135
300–305	150
325–330	165
345–350	175
370–375	190
400–405	205
425–430	220
445–450	230
470–475	245
500	260

Liquid Measure to Milliliters

¼ teaspoon	=	1.25 milliliters
½ teaspoon	=	2.5 milliliters
¾ teaspoon	=	3.75 milliliters
1 teaspoon	=	5.0 milliliters
1¼ teaspoons	=	6.25 milliliters
1½ teaspoons	=	7.5 milliliters
1¾ teaspoons	=	8.75 milliliters
2 teaspoons	=	10.0 milliliters
1 tablespoon	=	15.0 milliliters
2 tablespoons	=	30.0 milliliters

Liquid Measure to Liters

¼ cup	=	0.06 liters
½ cup	=	0.12 liters
¾ cup	=	0.18 liters
1 cup	=	0.24 liters
1¼ cups	=	0.3 liters
1½ cups	=	0.36 liters
2 cups	=	0.48 liters
2½ cups	=	0.6 liters
3 cups	=	0.72 liters
3½ cups	=	0.84 liters
4 cups	=	0.96 liters
4½ cups	=	1.08 liters
5 cups	=	1.2 liters
5½ cups	=	1.32 liters

Recipe Index

Craft Index